EVENLEY . N

How our village has evolved between the Second World War and the present day and the Characters who contributed to that change.

Also published by Evenley Residents Association

ASPECTS OF EVENLEY

The history of Evenley, a small village in Northamptonshire, from pre Roman times to the Second World War.
It shows how it has developed over time, has been shaped by its past and finishes with a suggested walk round the village.

TALES OF EVENLEY

The memoires of Cicely Spencer and Bill Buggins of the life and changes in the village during their lifetime.

DISCLAIMER
This book brings together facts about the village of Evenley from around 1945 to the present day and is about those who were involved with the changes. Any views and opinions collated in this book are those of the characters of Evenley and do not represent the views of the ERA or its members

ISBN No. 978 -0-9543808-2-3

Produced by Robert Boyd, Printing and Publishing Services
260 Colwell Drive, Witney, Oxon. OX28 5LW

SPONSORS

We would particularly like to thank our Sponsors for their generous donations which have made a major contribution to covering the costs of publishing this book.

David & Barbara Bailey
John & Sheila Bailey
Andrew & Mary Bullock
Lord Boswell
David & Hilary Brooke
David & Olive Bush
Chris & Marian Chippendale
Jessica Church
David & Heather Connolly
Paul & Angie Crompton
Bob & Janet Cropley
Richard & Kate Darby
Evenley Cricket Club
Evenley Parish Council
Evenley Red Lion
Evenley Village Shop
Mike & Jo Ewens
Nigel Fox
Stuart & Wendy Freestone
Jeremy & Josceline Hebblethwaite
Steve Hogarth & Lynette Petersen
Tony & Margaret Hollis
Roy & Julia Jennings
Bref & Jill Kelly
Barrie & Jean Morgan
Old Hall Bookshop, Brackley
Kevin & Carrie O'Regan
Susan Parker
Mark & Lisa Proffitt
Lyn Pyatt & Neal Umney
Charles & Frances Reader
Stephen Reid
Brian & Myrtle Robbins
Tony & Joyce Stevens
Richard & Terry Stopford
Michael & Liz Anne Wainwright
Walford & Round, Brackley
Chris & Emma Wightman

ACKNOWLEDGMENTS

This book could not have been produced without the input and help of many people in the village. We are particularly grateful to those who have contributed to the design, who have written their own stories, who have lent us photographs and those who have given us information about the village and their ancestors. The front and back cover drawings are by Sheila Bailey.

CONTENTS

LIST OF ILLUSTRATIONS

INTRODUCTION

After publishing "Aspects of Evenley" in 2002 and "Tales of Evenley" in 2005 we thought our work was done!

However after talking to people in the village and thinking about the way that Evenley had changed over the years we realised that there was one more important gap in our history to fill.

Hence "Characters of Evenley" evolved, showing how our village has grown since the Second World War.

You may think that this title is somewhat irrelevant but a village consists of two things; on the one hand its organisations, such as its Parish Council, Church, Shop, Pub, Residents Association and its Societies and Clubs.

However, on the other hand, and more important, there are the people who contributed to the creation and development of these organisations, businesses and clubs.

Many of these Characters are sadly no longer with us. However they, with their present day successors, have made Evenley what it is today. There are also other Characters and Evenley families who have, in their different ways, contributed very significantly to our advancement, admiration and amusement. Some are written about as individuals and others appear in the text about the organisation with which they are or were involved.

Although the 1940s are the starting point for the book much that has happened since then has had its origin before that time so we have drawn on the earlier history of the village, where relevant, in order to produce a picture which reflects both continuity and change.

It has been a difficult job combining these two interrelated themes but we hope that this book records the changes accurately and gives a broad and interesting picture of the village today.

But, more important, we hope that it pays tribute to the people who brought the changes about and to the large number of talented people who live in the village.

R.J.H. & J.M.H.

THE EMERGENCE OF EVENLEY AS A VILLAGE

The village of Evenley would probably not now exist without Evenley Hall; or worse, be a suburb of Brackley, some two miles away.

The Hall was built in about 1740 and came into the ownership of the Pierrepont family in 1803. The Allen family became owners in 1890 and re-built the Hall in 1897 after a disastrous fire.

From 1740 until 1936, when Major Allen died, the Hall and the Evenley Hall Estate had been in continuous private ownership.

It was then decided to sell off the Hall and the Estate in separate lots and the sale was completed in 1938.

The village's role up to that point had been to provide services for the Hall and the surrounding farms with the Hall's staff living mainly around the Green.

With the introduction of a substantial number of private purchasers and, therefore, owners, Evenley entered its second role as a much more broadly based village in its own right.

This and the changes in society which came with the Second World War were the beginnings of the development of the character of Evenley over the next seventy years to make it the village it is now.

EVENLEY SINCE WORLD WAR II

The sale of the Evenley Hall Estate and the end of the Second World War with its social changes are therefore the starting points for our book.

The earlier history of Evenley (Evenlai in the Domesday Book) has been covered to a large extent in our two books, "Aspects of Evenley" and "Tales of Evenley". However it is worth recording the actual entry in the Domesday Book of 1086 which is, in modern phraseology:-

"Otbert holds of Walter 2 hides in Evenlai. There is land for five ploughs. There are 4 ploughs, with 10 villans and 5 bordars. It was worth 30s; now 40s. The same man holds of Walter 1½ hides and the fifth part of a hide. There is land for 4 ploughs. In desmesne are 1½ (ploughs) with 1 slave; and 5 villans and 3 borders having 1½ ploughs. There is a mill rendering 2s. It was worth 20s.; now 40s. This land belongs to Evenlai."

Make of this what you will!

At the end of the Second World War Evenley was still, primarily, a village dependent on agriculture. It was surrounded by farms, as it is today, but then they and Evenley Hall were the main or only source of employment for the villagers.

The village itself was, of course, much smaller and the main houses were around the Green (except for the east side), the Manor, the Vicarage, some of Church Lane and Evenley Hall.

The Parish

The village is the centre of the Parish of Evenley which extends to include part of the Mercedes/Brawn GP complex (formerly Honda) just outside Brackley, the Tesco car park, but not the store itself, part of the RAF Croughton base, Evenley Fields farm, the Barley Mow, the farms along the Buckingham road, Evenley Hall and Bowling Green.

Evenley is right at the south-western tip of Northamptonshire and is in one of the largest parishes in the county. The Parish is approximately 3200 acres in size and the boundary has not been changed, at least since the war.

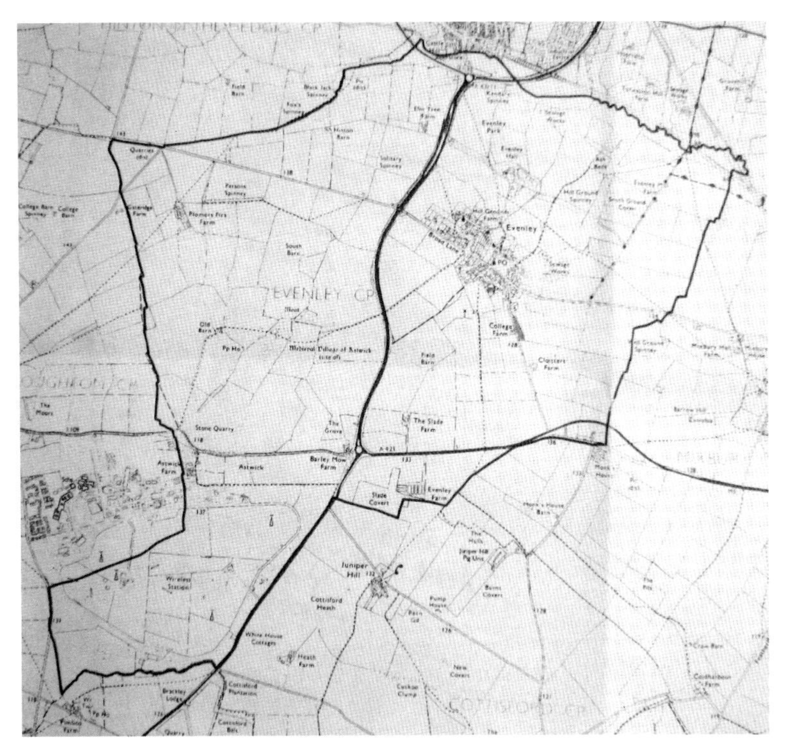

The boundary of the Parish

Parts of the Parish outside the village

Whilst this book is very largely about the village of Evenley it is useful to see the village in a wider context, particularly as some of the contributors to Evenley's emergence have lived outside the village but in the Parish.

Even so it may seem strange that, in particular, the Mercedes/Brawn GP complex, the Tesco car park and part of the RAF Croughton base are in the Parish but this is because the Parish boundaries were drawn before these developments were conceived.

The Great Ouse

Part of the Parish boundary was set as the bank of the Great Ouse, known in Celtic as "The ditch of muddy water"

In fact the source itself of this river is not far away from the Parish. We first pick it up as the rather modest ditch between the Tesco car park and the store itself where it flows towards the east.

The Great Ouse flowing beside the Tesco car park

To quote " when it leaves Northants it skirts a mile or so of the Oxfordshire border before beginning its journey through Buckinghamshire, Bedfordshire, Huntingdonshire, Cambridgeshire, the Isle of Ely and Norfolk to the Wash"

In that journey it becomes a major river 150 miles long. So you can see how significant the Tesco car park is to the ecology of the Midlands and East Anglia!

A unique Parish

When we include these outlying parts of the Parish we see that very few, if any, other parishes in Britain can house such variety; a supermarket (nearly), part of a highly successful Formula 1 base, (including the wind tunnel), part of the right bank of the Great Ouse, one of the three most important US communications bases in the world, (including Second World War fighter pens), the Barley Mow (a Roman garrison building dating back to about 200 A.D.), a medieval village (since destroyed), a quarry, Bowling Green, (with a long history), and, of course, a number of farms as well as the listed building, Evenley Hall.

The Mercedes / Brawn GP complex

Part of the communications base in the Parish

A 43

Bisecting all this is the A43 which runs from Northampton to the M40. It provides a valuable connection between the M1 and the A34 which takes it to the docks in Southampton. The dualling of the road also incorporating the Brackley bypass was completed in 2002 to the delight of Evenley residents who well remember the massive traffic jams outside Brackley, particularly on a Friday evening. The Parish also houses an overnight stopping place for lorries between the Evenley roundabout and the Barley Mow. The roundabout at the top of Broad Lane was installed after the dualling and as a result of accidents which had occurred and has made the exit from Evenley much safer.

Location

Evenley is in a slight dip in the surrounding landscape, with the Green being about the lowest point, apart from the ponds at the beginning of Bicester Hill. It is 400 ft. (122m.) above sea level but as the land rises up Broad Lane, Bicester Hill and towards Evenley Hall the height of the land increases by about 30-40 feet.

Evenley is more or less in the middle of England, nevertheless it is only about 80 miles (130km.) as the crow flies to the nearest sea, which is the Wash.

Proposed transfer to Oxfordshire

In 1970 the Redcliffe-Maud report proposed that Evenley and Croughton should be transferred from Northamptonshire to Oxfordshire. This was strongly opposed "as it was felt that the rates were higher in Oxfordshire, the roads worse and that the strong relationship which had been built up with Northamptonshire County Council would be lost."

It was said that "Evenley had no wish to become part of the tail end of some other county" – but one can but note that it is at the tail end of Northamptonshire!

Not everyone has abided by the decision to remain in Northamptonshire as certain developers have advertised their houses as being in Oxfordshire, thus attempting to enhance their selling price.

Bowling Green

Bowing Green is unusual in that the major part of it is in Northamptonshire and a minor part in Oxfordshire. It really is at the tail end of the county. It consists of four houses, one of which, Monks House, existed in 1662 and has a datestone recording 1683. It is thought that it was the home of George Monck, 1st Duke of Albemarle who, amongst other things fought on the Royalist side in the Civil War, much of which took place in this area and is referred to in more detail in "Aspects of Evenley".

There is a rumour that there was a tunnel from Monks House to a Castle next to Mixbury Church so that General Monck could escape from the Parliamentarians, if necessary.

Parliamentary Constituency

Evenley was in the Parliamentary Constituency of South Northamptonshire from 1832 until 1918 when it became part of the new Constituency of

Daventry. However in 1950 Evenley was returned to the South Northamptonshire Constituency only to be returned again to Daventry in 1974. Moreover the Boundary Commission has now decided that Evenley will be in the revised South Northamptonshire Constituency for the election in 2010, although it is now possible that it will become part of yet another constituency if the referendum due in 2011 is approved.

Evenley has been represented in Parliament by four MPs since the war, the latest being Tim Boswell, who retired at the 2010 election after 22 years as a member and is now Lord Boswell of Aynho. He was succeeded by Andrea Leadsom. The village is also in the East Midlands constituency of the European Parliament. The constituency is represented by five MEPs.

Planning and the Conservation area

Evenley itself is "identified as a Restricted Infill Village in the South Northamptonshire Local Plan. The residential policies make provision for appropriate small scale infilling within the village confines".

The area around the Green and most of Church Lane was designated a Conservation Area in 1968 with consequent restrictions on development in order to maintain its character.

Population

There was no Census of population in 1941 but the censuses of 1931 and 1951 give Evenley Parish residents of 334 and 382 respectively so the population then was probably about 360 people. This had risen to about 450 in 1968 and a present day population of about 600.

Building

The village began to expand with the building of nine council houses in School Lane in 1947. Some of the houses on the east side of the Green were built soon after the war but the majority were built in the 1960s. This was followed by the first major private development, Lawyers Close, also in the 1960s.

Fields around the village

Around the village, there were a number of fields and roads with interesting and unusual names, the origin of which is often unknown, some of which have since been built on, for example:-

Backside Field – now Church Leys,

Backside Gardens, then "the allotments" – now Spencer Close,

Bone Hill – now School Lane
Bottom Butterfields
Bowling Green
Dog kennel Piece
Dutch Oven – so called because of the shape of the field
First Rudge Way
Hoo Titty
Lion Close
Lawyers Close
Puddleduck, which is behind Boughton Terrace,

Railway Lines

Two railway lines cross the North East corner of the Parish, both of which are currently disused. These are:-

The London and Northwestern Railway from Bletchley via Buckingham, Brackley (St James's) and Banbury.

The Great Central Railway main line from Marylebone via Brackley (Central) to Rugby, Leicester, Nottingham and Sheffield.

Interestingly the Government Report on a high speed link between London and Birmingham stated in relation to the route ..."following the largely preserved track-bed of the former Great Central Railway until Brackley..."so it is possible that we will have up to 10 high speed trains an hour, each way, passing through the Parish sometime in the second quarter of the century.

Airport

In 1968 there was a plan to site London's third Airport at Silverstone which would have badly affected Evenley. This was vigorously opposed by local people who formed action groups and also by the Campaign for the Preservation of Rural England through its Northamptonshire, Buckinghamshire and Oxfordshire branches. In March 1969 the good news came that the airport would be sited at Cublington. Silverstone, and therefore Evenley, was reprieved, later in favour of the expansion of Stanstead.

Aircraft

Evenley is a quiet village except when there is no wind or when it is northerly; then the traffic on the A43 makes itself heard.

It also gets a variable amount of noise from aircraft. The most significant is the sound of low flying helicopters going to and returning from Silverstone, which is set to continue for at least another sixteen years. There is also some noise from high flying commercial aircraft from Midland airports. However most of the traffic on normal days is from private planes, including a biplane reminiscent of a Gloster Gladiator, microlites and a motorised glider. Until the early 1990s there used to be the roar of F 1-11s which, some villagers believed, lined up on the Church spire for the final approach to landing at Upper Heyford.

THE GREEN

The Green, which has the War Memorial, the Shop, the Village Hall and The Red Lion on or around it is undoubtedly the centre of Evenley. It also has the distinction of being the finest village green and the best cricket pitch in Northamptonshire and probably one of the largest village greens in England.

Having such a centre to the village is an enormous benefit because, unlike strip developments, it brings a major degree of cohesion and community to village life. This benefits those visiting the Shop, Post Office, Village Hall, Pub and friends around the Green (including those gardening at the front of their houses!) and gives corresponding benefits to those visited.

Venue

It is the venue for the village cricket teams, the early August motor cycle run, the August bank holiday Church Fayre, the fun run, football kickarounds, cricket nets, rounders matches, french cricket, kite flying, rocket and model aeroplane launching, emergency helicopter landings and the occasional golf practice. It has even been rumoured to be a collection point for a parachutist testing free fall for the SAS!

These activities do not usually give rise to risks for the householders except that windowpanes and motor cars have met cricket balls on occasions and exceptional shots have even been hit over houses into back gardens – always when Evenley has been batting – of course!

Ownership of the Green

The Green was purchased by the Parish Council, who still own it, from a Mrs Blakiston, who lived in Boughton Close, in 1961 for £100. It comprised 2.925 acres then and probably slightly less now with the continual erosion of the verges by passing vehicles. It was registered as a Village Green in 1968.

Houses around the Green

The Green was laid out in its present form by the Pierreponts in about 1850 and included a road from the Red Lion to the opposite corner so that horse drawn carriages could more easily reach Evenley Hall.

The houses on the south, west and north sides are all very old and part of the Evenley Conservation Area; only the houses on the east side were built after 1945.

On the west side is Dormer Row, a row of what were originally the Pierreponts workmens' cottages and one now regarded as an important part of the Evenley Conservation Area. The two exceptional features of the row are that the back gardens are largely offset so that one's view is mainly of one's neighbour's garden. Even more bizarre the front doors were all at the back supposedly because Mrs Pierrepont did not wish to see her servants gossiping as she drove past in her carriage. Perhaps an early "Character" of Evenley, although not by modern day standards!

Dormer Row

Other features of the older houses and cottages on the Green include unusual roofs with distinctive bands of alternating red and black tiles and a few Yorkshire sideways sliding sash windows. It is not known how they came to be a feature of a Northamptonshire village! A more detailed description of the houses round the Green can be found in our publication "Aspects of Evenley".

Old Post Office Row

Continuing clockwise we come to what used to be known as Post Office Row including a mixture of private housing, Housing Association (formerly Council) houses and the Village Shop and Post Office.

Guy Fawkes Night

Next there is one house with a thatched roof which stands at right angles to the Green next to the shop. It is here that a village custom met its end. Traditionally, a bonfire had always been built on the Green on Guy Fawkes Night. One unhappy year a rogue rocket set fire to its thatch and the Parish Council decided that bonfires on the Green were too great a risk to houses. The location for the fireworks was then moved to the Pocket Park but met with "Health and Safety" problems so it was moved to a field behind Lawyers Close where, perhaps appropriately, it "fizzled out."

The Thatched House as it is today

The south side of the Green, as you pass the Red Lion, has a row of older houses and used to be nicknamed Coppings Row.

The road through the Green and the Stocks

The road across the Green was originally so that horse drawn vehicles had easy acess to Evenley Hall. It was turfed over in 1962 so that cricket could be played on the Green, having lost its pitch on Church Leys. You can sometimes see the tracks of the road both from the ground and, more conspicuously from an aerial photograph.

There was one objector to the turfing over, Walter Gascoigne, who complained to the Court but was unsuccessful. Another objector was unhappy about the abolition of the short cut, saying "I can get in an extra pint at the Red Lion if I come across that way"!

The Stocks were at the north east corner. These were taken down and burned in about 1850 when the Green was laid out. It is not known when they were last used or who the occupier and his or her crime was.

The Green from the air

Earthworks

The Green has been partly dug up on at least two occasions. First for the laying of electricity cables when they were put underground and secondly when at least one hillock was removed to improve the outfield for cricket, perhaps reducing the advantage of local knowledge.

Mowing the Green

The Parish Council is responsible for the mowing of the Green and Peter Franklin and Ray Roycroft did this vital job for many years. It is now contracted out. The Green has not always had the benefit of modern machinery for its upkeep as the photograph beside shows.

Dorothy Roycroft taking a sheep for a walk

The benches on the Green

There are eleven benches round the Green, eight of which are in memory of individuals. Starting from the Shop and going clockwise these are

Vaughan Jones
Jack Chapman
Reg and Betty Copping
John and Jo Morgan,
(landlords of the Red Lion from 1971-1985)

David Greatbatch
Ken and Betty Ames
Samuel Goodman
Ron Jell

The dedications reflect the individual's contribution to and love of the village and, as you would expect, also a love of cricket.
There was also a tablet, to Leonard Warren, Chairman of the PC in the late 1960s and a Rural District and County Councillor, probably on the seat on the elm stump which was by the Village Hall.

Helicopter landing ground

As well as all the sporting activities the Green has also been host to two recent helicopter landings.

One helicopter was unable to return to base because of a storm. It landed on the east side and the crew were promptly invited to tea in a nearby house before taking off again when the weather was clear!

The other was for a medical emergency when, in fact, the person concerned was taken away by ambulance

Two helicopters in different emergencies

The trees on the Green

In the halcyon '60s before Dutch Elm disease struck the Green was stage to a cast of "Immemorial Elms" – five in number – the remains of one, like a decay ridden tooth, remained on the North East corner until recently, testament to the rot proof quality of elmwood.

The Queen's Jubilee plaque

Subsequent replanting was a miscellany – there remained the ubiquitous Sycamore and two Limes, part of the Pierrepont legacy. Some of the new trees were planted in memoriam of deceased relatives, some as a delightful whim; one, a beech, to celebrate the Queen's Silver Jubilee. Almost all, except for one on the Green, survived the great storm of 1987.

Virulent disease

But how sad to reflect that twice in half a century, our trees on the Green have suffered as a result of a virulent disease introduced to England on imported timber. Around the millennium it became apparent that Horse Chestnuts were developing bark lesions swiftly followed by death as the result of a scourge, Phytophera ramorum, and although Pink Chestnuts seem more resistant all four of these were deemed to be infected and condemned.

Opportunity

One has to look on death as an opportunity for life in the natural world, so the Parish Council and the Residents Association initiated a re-planting scheme, financed also by a concert by Nigel Fox's band, The Montanas, and very generous donations from the village. Democracy to the fore, a questionnaire was sent round naming eight suitable species, and inviting a vote for the most popular.

The trees chosen

There was a great response resulting in the planting of a double White Cherry (the single form occurring naturally hereabout) on the west side, with a Tulip Tree nearby on the south-west corner. Opposite the Pub, the Maple called

Princeton Gold whose spring display of acid green moderates as summer waxes, and on the east side a Sweet Chestnut which met with a seam of rock, so we hope its native tendency to cope with poor, well drained ground will stand it in good stead.

The new trees and some of the older ones have had daffodils planted round them by the Gardening Society and the Residents Association making the coming of Spring more evident.

Heritage

The stature and longevity of trees make them a natural part of Evenley's heritage and we expect that the new recruits will blend with their mature cousins and become a part of it.

An oak tree on the Green in different seasons

So the village is blessed with a wonderful Green which acts as the centre-piece of its life with many of its facilities and activities focused around it.

ACTIVITIES ON AND AROUND THE GREEN

The Green is there for all the village to use, within practical limits, for sporting activities. It tends to be dominated from May to August by cricket, for which the village is well known.

However, apart from Saturday afternoons and some Sundays in that period it is widely used for quite a variety of other sporting activities. These include football kickarounds, cricket nets and rounders matches and even the occasional golf practice.

Cricket

Cricket has always been important in Evenley. It was originally played at Evenley Hall, then on land at Rectory Farm on a pitch which was then taken for the Church Leys housing development. Finally it moved to the Green, the centre of Evenley, and is played on one of the best wickets in the South Northamptonshire leagues.

Mike Bosher, the current Chairman of the Club, came to the village in 1978 and joined the first team. He provided the first sponsorship for the Club and became at different times Secretary, Treasurer and Chairman.

He has worked with Mo Greatbatch, a strong supporter, who has been Treasurer and also did the teas before and after the Red Lion became the focus for refreshment, a mantle taken up by her daughter, Biddy.

In 1997 the Club started to raise its game and subsequently the first eleven went on to win the Premier League Championship in 2001, 2002, 2004, 2005, 2006 and 2007. They finishing runners up in 2008, 2009 and 2010.

In the 2010 season Anthony Romaine was captain of the first eleven, which is in the South Northants Premier Division. Chris Scott was captain of the second eleven in Division Two and Andrew Reader captain of the third eleven in Division Four. Michael Peyton-Bruhl was in charge of the juniors.

All matches are played on the limited over basis. The first team plays 45 over matches with the second and third teams playing 40 overs

The Club has substantial support in the village and has an amazing 100 or more Vice Presidents, a number of whom are also ball sponsors for individual matches.

There have been many exciting and, indeed, epic moments in the life of the Club to win a match or to tie up winning the league.

Off the pitch one of the more unusual events was the dinner dance where the renowned Times cricket correspondent and BBC commentator Christopher Martin Jenkins, who had a connection locally through Winchester House in Brackley, was Guest of Honour and made a hilarious speech.

Another was the poem written by Graham Wiblin telling the story of an epic Evenley innings in1984 against Long Crendon. It is unfortunately too long to reproduce here but can be found on the Club's website, along with all fixtures, results and much more. The poem is also on display in the Red Lion.

Many Evenley residents have contributed to the success of the teams both on and off the field, including:-

Dick Vernon, President, who took over from Bill Woodgate
George Sharp, NCC. wicket keeper and now umpire, first class
David Greatbatch, wicket keeper
Peter Franklin, all rounder
Richard Franklin who also cut the grass before Peter took over.
Graham, Freddie and Jim Harman
Vaughan and Jamie Martin
Reg Copping and sons:-
Roger, Trevor, Steve & Martin (aka Snaky)
Nigel Fox
Chris Scott
Ian Moodie

And, of course, the Management Committee under Mike Bosher and his predecessors.

Cricketing awards (and hairstyles) from 1975

From left to right, Vaughan Martin, Scott Hazell, Graham Harman, John Dye, David Robinson and Peter Franklin

The first eleven (minus one) in 2010

Football

Football has had a varied reception on the Green. At present there is one moveable goal which allows for shooting practice but not a full "so many a side" game.

Past problems

In the past it was not so flexible. In 1968 the children of the village ran errands, washed cars and did other jobs to buy wood to make goal posts which were then erected on the Green, holes being dug for them.

The goalposts had only been up a few weeks when the secretary of the Parish Council took them down and locked them away in the Village Hall. This was as a result of a decision at the AGM of the Parish Council because people said they were "unsightly"

The village shop keeper, Ernie Holah said "The children got a team together two years ago. They carried manure, washed cars, dug people's gardens and ran a weekly raffle to pay for the kit and the goalposts. They even dug the holes for the posts to go in – and now they have had their own property pulled down in front of their eyes. It is disgraceful!"

The children sent a petition to the Parish Council signed by 60 villagers demanding their posts be replaced.

There was considerable argument in the village and the Parish Council agreed to hold an emergency meeting to discuss the matter.

There was a meeting attended by 80 villagers and children and it was decided that the posts should be left on the Green from September until April inclusively and then taken down for the summer. A group of villagers – Mr G W Gray, Mr. David Greatbatch, Mr. A L Hunt, Mr. S V Jones and Mr. T. Blackmore volunteered to maintain the posts.

The Bill Lacey Memorial Motor Cycle Run

A large number of motor cycles have gathered around the Green, by the Red Lion, on the first Sunday in August for each of the last twenty years.

This is for the Bill Lacey Memorial Run in memory of Bill Lacey who lived in Evenley, broke ten motor cycling world records and won the "Motor Cycle Cup" all in one day.

The Large capacity tank is virtually
the only deviation from standard

Bill Lacey with his winning motor cycle

The Run was established by Ann, his daughter, who also lives in Evenley. The Run commemorates not only Bill's world records but also his remarkable life in the world of engineering and motor cycle racing.

Bill was born in 1901 and started his adult life by being apprenticed to an engineering firm in Slough and then went to work for a garage in Maidenhead where he built motor cycles for hill climbs. From there he went to Brooklands to race and became interested in trying for records which involved him going to France to the Montlhery "Saucer" circuit.

The record breaking run

However on the 1st of August 1928 at Brooklands he achieved his ambition. On a Grindlay-Peerless 498cc."Square" with a J.A.P. engine he covered 103.3 miles in one hour to break these ten records.

One hour	1000cc. class		
One hour	750cc. class	50 miles	750cc.class
One hour	500cc. class	50 miles	500cc. class
100 miles	1000cc. class		
100 miles	750cc. class	100km.	750cc.class
100 miles	500cc. class	100km.	500cc.class

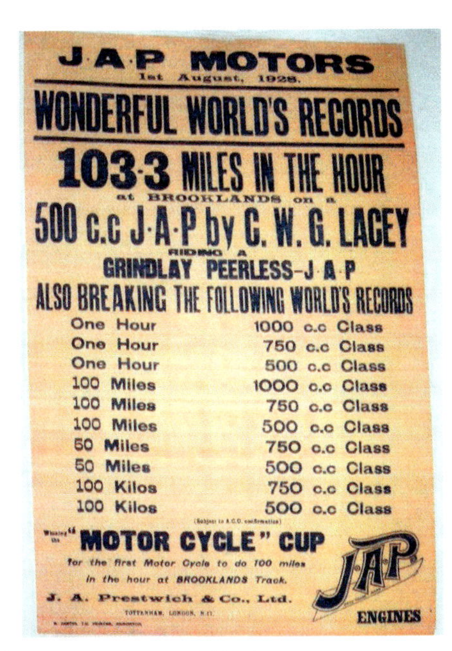

Ann had Bill's records printed on a T Shirt

The Motor Cycle Cup

With the same run he also won the "Motor Cycle Cup" for the first motor cycle to cover 100 miles in one hour, a task regarded by most racing experts as impossible, because of the restrictions imposed at Brooklands and the dangerous nature of its surface.

One consequence of these records was that there was a demand for replicas of the machine on which he had been so successful. He made a number of them at the request of private buyers and there are also replicas in the Brooklands museum and in the Motor Cycle museum near the N.E.C. in Birmingham.

His own machine shop

Bill started his own machine shop in the late thirties to make parts and modifications for bikes and cars. When the war started he was asked to do some machining of important parts for Radar installations which were becoming crucial to the defence of Britain. He also joined the Fire Brigade.

After the war was over his business continued and he also became involved in making parts for film cameras for J. Arthur Rank and solving the problems of installing them. This meant that he was often on film sets despite the unions' "Closed Shop" rule. A tribute to both his engineering skills and his tact.

The last part of his career involved setting up another machine shop which, by chance, got him back into the racing world as he was asked to rebuild an M.V. Augusta which Stan Hailwood had bought from John Surtees. At this point Ann joined him and they worked on bikes and on car engines. The work on car engines was for Rob Walker, Bruce MacLaren, John Surtees, U.D.T. and Yeoman Credit. Clients came from Australia, South Africa, France and Switzerland as well as Britain.

During his career he worked with and made friends with Stirling Moss, Mike and Stan Hailwood, Geoff Duke, John Hartle, Phil Read and many others.

The Memorial Run

When Bill died in 1989 Ann asked Banbury Vintage Motor Cycle Club (VMCC) if they would do a memorial run for her father. They had already filled their dates for 1990 but said that they would come on the first Sunday in August in 1991.

On that day Banbury, North Cotswold, Northampton and Oxford VMCCs and the Velocette owners club came to Evenley. The Red Lion overflowed and all agreed that the run should happen every year. The meeting has increased in size over the years (about 250 motor cycles at the last estimate) and there is a mixture of vintage and modern cycles.

Some of the participants in the Memorial Run in 2009

The Memorial Run is one of the unmissable Evenley events and a lasting tribute to a great racer, a highly skilled engineer and a most popular man.

The Village Fun Run

The Fun Run was started in about 1988 by Ron Jell and others and normally takes place whenever there is a summer Fete. The run is open to all comers and there are entrants from Brackley and our surrounding villages. There are typically up to 50 entrants. The run starts from the north east corner of the Green, goes past the sewage works, on towards Hill Ground Spinney, turns right and then skirts Evenley Wood Garden, then doubles back along Mill Lane and back to the Green. The course is two miles long or for masochists a second circuit makes it four miles.

In recent years the run has been organised by Ian and Maggie Hicks and Chris Ellis. There are nine awards for running, including for the fastest circuit, the fastest double circuit, the best performance by an Evenley resident, fastest lady and medals and certificates for children. There is even a fancy dress award.

August Fairs

The first August fair was initiated by the Cricket Club and there have been a number of different fairs on the Green over the years. The most recent has been the August Bank Holiday Fayre in aid of Church funds. These took place in 2007 and 2008 and have been most ably run by Pat Reeves and her committee.

As well as the Fun Run there was an immensely popular Dog Show (a spectator heard a little girl say to her mother "can I please take a dog round the course" to which the mother replied "we don't have a dog, why not take your father?") There was also a barbecue organised by the Cricket Club, a visit by local alpacas, a plant stall, bric-a-brac, tombola, a produce stall, books and discs, a rare breeds stall, face painting, toys and two games run by the Residents Association.

The amount of money raised for Church funds was just under £4000 in 2008.

The Fayre

Vintage Tractors

On a Sunday in October 2009 a great procession of tractors circled the Green and came to a halt facing the Red Lion. It transpired that this was one of several outings of the Bicester Vintage Tractor Club. Each time they do a tour of neighbouring villages, stopping at a pub for a little light refreshment before moving on and returning to base for a celebratory meal. In all there were thirty one tractors ranging in age from 1912 to 1970 and over £400 was raised for charity on this occasion.

Some of the vintage tractors

THE WAR MEMORIAL

The War Memorial is in the centre of the south side of the Green and was paid for by members of the village to commemorate the Evenley men who lost their lives in the First World War. Strangely their names were not listed on the memorial at the time but Bill Buggins gave the names of five of them in his history.

Happily there were no Evenley casualties in the Second World War.

In about 1979 there was a minor ruction in the village as some people felt that a plaque marking the Second World War should be added to the memorial.

Dick Bright, Clerk to the Parish Council, said "It's true that no one from the village died in the 1939-45 war. And there are people in the village who think that the memorial should be left as it is, with the names of the fallen in the First War. But more recently there have been newcomers in the community who have had different ideas".

As the Parish Council failed to resolve the dispute between the two factions it was decided to hold a ballot of the more than 200 residents.

The War Memorial

Those in favour of a reference to the Second World War were successful and the memorial now reads

The Great War 1914-1918
Lest we forget
1939-1945

In 2007 it was decided to clean and restore the Memorial financed by donations from the village and a grant. At the same time it was noticed that none of the names were on the Memorial. It was also noticed that there had in fact been six casualties in the earlier war as was recorded in the Church.

The newly restored Memorial now carries the names of all the six Evenley men who were killed in the First World War.

They were:

Ernest Chartwell
Herbert George
Thomas Holton
Ernest Pratt
Thomas Reynolds
Michael Leigh Russel

Every year on Armistice Sunday the road in front of the Memorial is closed for a short service of commemoration, now led by Carrie O'Regan, at which the two minute silence is observed and the Chairman of the Parish Council reads out the names of the fallen.

THE VILLAGE SHOP

The Village Shop and Post Office is at 23 The Green, part of Old Post Office Row, and is well placed to be a focus for information, meeting up with friends and, of course, shopping. It serves Mixbury and other villages as well as Evenley.

The building

The deeds of the building indicate that part of the original fabric dates back to 1530. The present building was probably built by the Pierreponts in the 1870s. It has been used as a wheelwright's workshop and a malt-house barn. From 1925 the building was used as the Men's Clubroom and Village Hall until 1966 when it was sold and became the present Shop.

The Village Shop

Earlier shops

Evenley had a number of small shops before this one. The cottage on the corner of the Hollows was an off licence and then a shop. There was then a small shop also with an off licence in a cottage, since demolished, on the corner of School Lane. It was from this shop that the then licensee of the Red Lion, who was in dispute with the brewery, bought many of his supplies!

Owners

Post war owners have included Ernie Holah and Vic and Jenny Smith. Today's shop was opened by Major Randall Hunter who also added the first floor flat. He was, undoubtedly one of the "Characters" of Evenley, not only because he did not recognise the afternoon, greeting everyone with a slightly crusty "Good Morning" regardless of the time of day. But, more important, he had the vision to open the shop and keep it going, thus creating one of the building blocks of the village. He retired in 1989 and the shop closed.

Russells of Evenley

Nick Russell – "Russells of Evenley" - and certainly a "Character", re-opened the shop on 1st April 1991 and the first day's takings were £59 which got it off to a promising start.

Nick, when proprietor of the Village Shop

He instituted the system of a reversible green and red board outside the shop for "open" and "closed", thus saving many inhabitants of the Green with failing memories from fruitless journeys.

Nick changed the nature of the shop to make it more "The "Mini Fortnums of Evenley" and also to serve the surrounding villages, particularly Mixbury.

A quotation about the shop at that time said "Well known to dinner party circuits, where else at the last minute could you buy a champagne bucket, fresh Parmesan cheese, smoked salmon, Royal Shrewsbury bacon or choose from 26 different varieties of tea?" Evenley seems to have benefited from the lack of forward planning by some!

Jesse Wyles was one of many customers and one of the more unusual. As she was disabled she would draw up in front of the Shop in her Mercedes and hoot. At this sound Nick would bustle out, receive her shopping list, and then fulfil it, no doubt including many of the ingredients for her famous meringues and tea parties.

Nick Russell and Suzanne Boffin, who helped him in the Shop, were highly commended for the Shop in the Calor Gas annual "best village shop" competition one year.

Transition

Nick left the village in 2004 to take up a place as a principal tenor at Worcester Cathedral. During his time in Evenley he had achieved many things, including earning the title of "Living National Treasure" from Country Life in 1998.

Nick Russell hosting the V.E.Day party on 8th May 1995

The Wainwrights and the Scaysbrooks combined to save the shop and Linda Scaysbrook ran it with Philip, her brother, until 2007 thus ensuring its survival.

Sandra Walker takes over

Sandra Walker then took it over. She steadily expanded its services to include, as well as a renewed emphasis on the basics, a flourishing newspaper and magazine business, flowers, dry cleaning, shoe repairs, key cutting, bread and pastries, special orders and many other things (including selling the Residents Association's books!) to meet so many of the needs of the village. Sandra has been helped by Kate and also by others. Kate's family came to the village in the 1960s.

The shop is combined with the Post Office and they make an economic unit provided they are well supported.

Sandra at the Post Office with Kate behind the counter

Sandra has little leisure time but was given a flight in a light aeroplane for a birthday present. Despite never having been in any plane before she bravely took the offer up. To prove she really had flown she took the photograph on page **19**.

THE POST OFFICE

The Post Office, which in the past has been both separate from the Shop and part of it, has had a number of homes, notably at No. 47 The Green during the war. It seems subsequently to have been lodged at other houses around the Green, including No. 54.

Decimalisation drama

On 15th February 1971 decimalisation came in. The staff at the Brackley Post Office went on strike as they had not been trained in decimalisation and the office was closed while the staff were trained.

The result of this was a considerable benefit to Evenley. Pensioners and mothers came from miles around to Evenley village shop to collect their pensions and family allowances. Ernest Holah, the shop keeper, said that people could hardly get into the shop to buy provisions because of the queue to collect pensions and benefits on Tuesdays and Fridays.

Mr. Holah was helped by Dick Bright, Evenley Parish Clerk, as it was too difficult for one man to cope with the extra work caused by the strike, as well as explaining decimalisation to those collecting pensions and benefits. His Post Office business normally involved about £400 per week. This rose to £5,800 being paid out and all this for £35 salary a week with no extra payment, except that he must have benefitted from purchases from the shop.

More recent events

The Post Office was part of the Shop in Randall Hunter's time but when the Shop closed in 1989 when Randall left the village the village refused to accept closure of the Post Office. It was operated from a utility room in a house on the east side of the Green by Vi Jones. It was then brought back into the Shop when Nick Russell restarted it.

One of Nick's first actions was to paint the post box green, the colour it had been when it was installed in Victorian times. It subsequently took three men to restore it to its contemporary red!

In Nick's time the Post Office flourished, not only in its primary role but also as an intellectual hotbed. The team of Nick, Suzanne and Alwyn Boffin came top in the Post Office Inter –Regional Quiz and indeed had the highest score in the country.

Sandra Walker becomes Postmistress

In 2007 when Sandra took over the running of the Shop she also became, first, an apprentice postmistress and then, after completing her training, the official Postmistress. Particular duties include weighing parcels and letters, selling stamps, insurance for packages and special delivery. She sells foreign currency, Postal Orders, Premium Bonds, Savings Accounts, provides forms for ISA's and licences for fishing. She does Business Banking, cash withdrawals, bill payments and many other things. The administration of all this has to be very precise.

THE RED LION

The Red Lion's facade is mid-Victorian but the back is much older. Next to the Red Lion, towards Mixbury, stood the Village Pound, for the locking up of law breakers. It has now been replaced by residential housing of a more permanent kind.

The Red Lion

History

The history of the Red Lion includes the rumour that the last man in England to be hanged for sheep stealing was arrested there, probably in 1832. More certain is the fact that Tony Lees, the landlord at the time of Neil Armstrong's landing on the moon in 1969, put a time capsule into the wall of the fireplace of the cottage bar. This contained a newspaper account of the landing, a set

of pre-decimal coins and the names of the landlord and the men who had done the alterations. Famous visitors include Prince Charles who used to drink there after hunting with the Bicester.
Since the war the Red Lion has had ten landlords.

Plum Warner
Tony and Lois Lees
John and Jo Morgan (1971-85)
Geoff and Mo Earles
Chris and Sonia Thomkins
Nick Robinson and Peter Holden
Mel and Lee Baxter
Mike Bosher, Ian and Lisa Moody and Charles and Martina

Hayley Hammond takes over
In early 2009 the lease of the Red Lion again became available and, complicated by a change of Brewery from Kensington to Marston's, was acquired by Hayley Hammond for a minimum period of five years. The Red Lion re-opened first for drinks on the 8th June, followed by light refreshments in July and a full "rustic" menu in August. However, sadly, things did not work out as Hayley and the village had hoped and the Red Lion closed in February 2010.

Paul and Angie to the rescue!
Following the closure Paul and Angie Crompton who had lived in the village for some eight years decided to take the Red Lion challenge on. Thus grasping the opportunity to secure the future of the pub and to return it to its former glory; a village pub run by villagers for the village - or at least that was the plan!

After signing a ten year deal with the Brewery and going through all the necessary steps to take possession, finally on 22nd February 2010 it belonged to them. They set themselves the target of opening on Friday 26th February; four days in which to turn an empty shell in to a warm and cosy, welcoming village pub. Quite a challenge to say the least notwithstanding the big task of re-building the window seats which had been removed by the previous tenant, much to the dismay of the whole village.

They achieved this task and Raymond opened the pub at 6pm on the 26th February, just as the carpenter was putting the last touches to the seats. It seemed like the whole village turned up for the opening and to say the opening night was a roaring success is a huge understatement.

They have since gone from strength to strength, re-furbishing the kitchen and opening with a locally sourced menu selling simple British food. They are particularly grateful to all the villagers who helped in the first week with cleaning, tidying and sorting and not forgetting the village support after the event without which they wouldn't have a business.

So all looks well set for the restoration of the Red Lion to its premier and necessary place in the life of Evenley after a worrying period when it was feared that the village would lose one of its most important features:-

"The Cricketing Inn on the Green".

Paul and Angie enjoying their work!

THE VILLAGE HALL

The School

The Village Hall was built in 1832 as the Church of England Village School and continued as such until 1962 when the School was closed and bought by the Parish Council for £1600.

Positioned at the South West corner of the Green it is the first major building anyone entering Evenley down Broad Lane sees and the road running down to it from the South-West is called School Lane. On important national days the Hall will have the Union Jack run up its flagpole

The flag flying on the Queen's official birthday

Next to the Hall is School House, or No. 2 The Green, which was the schoolmaster or schoolmistresses house and was built in 1869. There was a door, now blocked up, leading from the courtyard to the present day kitchen so that the principal could enter the School conveniently, or quickly if it was raining!

When the school was closed because classes had got too small the children went by bus to Brackley to 'Feed My Lambs' and then on to Magdalen College.

Former pupils

A number of former pupils still live in the village or nearby, including Ray Rycroft, David Rouse, Myrtle Robbins (nee Shepherd) and her brother Tom, Les Buggins, Michael Ford and Sheila Tanner. Cicely Spencer's grandson, Stephen Reid, remembers being made to stand in the corner!

The class of an unknown year, Ray front centre

The new role as the Village Hall

When the Parish Council bought the School in 1962 it was to enable it to take over the role of the old Club Room, which had been in the building which is now the Village Shop.

A lot of renovation was needed to make it fit for its new role as the Village Hall. The Parish Council is responsible for the upkeep of the exterior of the Hall and the Village Hall Management Committee, which is a charity, for the interior.

Activities covered

The Hall is and has been used for many formal meetings and activities; Parish Council, Polling Station, Residents Association, Sunday School and Church Services, the monthly lunch and ad hoc village meetings including to discuss the planning application for a wind turbine.

There are Wedding receptions, Birthday parties for adults and for children, Funeral teas, Concerts, Theatricals, Olde Tyme Music Hall, Casino evenings and Gigs to raise money for good causes like the replacing of four trees on the Green.

And finally there are club activities including; Women's Institute, Bridge Club, Bingo, Chess, Evergreens Club, Gardening Club, Film Club, Flower Club, Singing and Signing Baby Club, Table Tennis Club, Whist and Beetle Drives and Youth Club; activities such as Pilates and Yoga, a changing room for Cricket, an adjunct to the Green for the Church Fayre on rainy days and just about every other village activity.

Madeline Furnivall managed the bookings from 1989 until 2007. Mo Greatbatch has now taken on this responsibility.

One particular event which was reported in the Towcester and Brackley Advertiser on the sixth of August 1976 was a display of local crafts and collectors' pieces. The exhibition was organised by Barry Smith and these people exhibited

Harold Chenery	Hand beaten metal tea service
Barry Smith	Collection of horse brasses
Ted Cox	First day cover stamp collection
Jessie Wyles	Collection of over 100 china Dalmatian dogs
Olive Westlake	Leather jerkin and suede coat with hand knitted sleeves
Dick Bright	Tapestried cushion

This shows the wide variety of interests in the village and one of the many uses to which the Hall can be put.

Facilities upgraded

Accommodating all these activities as well as the requirements of the modern age has meant that there has had to be a fairly continuous upgrading of the facilities with, from to time, a "great leap forward".

Important improvements have been made to comply with the Equal Opportunities Acts, the Disabilities Discrimination Act 1995, Health and Safety with their requirement for Risk Assessments and with the Licensing Laws. One of these regulatory bodies even specified the typeface and typesize for notices – Arial 14 and 12!

All this has put a considerable burden on the Management Committee and the individuals who have, voluntarily, carried out or supervised much of the work.

The things which needed doing were to create a changing room, adding showers, making a new kitchen, new flooring and ceiling in the main room, improving cloakroom facilities, new heating and improved entrance, particularly for the disabled.

Fund raising

Raising the money to pay for all this was a massive task and was spread over several years ending with a Millennium Grant. Ken Ames and David Harvey took on the challenge and in the end they raised a total of £90,000.

Not content with that it was then decided to replace the existing garage used for storage of equipment for the youth club etc. with a new building and a covered link to the Hall. The car park was also to be resurfaced. This was to cost in excess of £20,000 which was not helped by the contractor going into administration owing the committee £3500 for a VAT refund.

Donors

The money for these two projects came from fundraising in the village by Ken and David, the Committee, the Lottery Fund, South Northants Council, Northants County Council, Tesco, Brackley Co-Op, Lloyds TSB and Barclaycard.

The Hall now

The Hall now has a main room, a smaller room, a fully equipped kitchen, a changing room, the usual services and car parking. Donations of the cooker and the dishwasher have added to the facilities available to those hiring the Hall. As a result of the vision and hard work of the committee under Ian Mackway, Alex Crisp, Jeff Peyton-Bruhl and the Treasureship of Tony Hollis we now have, probably, the finest Village Hall in the County, along with the finest Village Green!

THE CHURCH

The Church of St George in Evenley was built at the instigation of Mrs Pierrepont in 1864/65 as a memorial to her husband. It was built on the foundations of a 12th century church which, although according to rumour, was burned down, was almost certainly pulled down as it was in a state of decay.

The only remaining medieval feature is a timber late mediaeval screen, with a central doorway flanked with cusped lights, which now stands in front of the tower arch.

The church interior consists of a chancel, nave, aisles, trancepts, south porch, organ chamber, a peal of five bells, a tower and a clock with chimes. There are seats for 240 people.

The Altar fronts were made by people in the village. The first was a white one made in memory of Dick Bright, which was finished by Carrie O'Regan and Margo Buttery. The other three a green, a purple and a red one were made by Carrie in memory of Molly Bright, Dick's wife.

The Church of St. George

St George

St George, the son of wealthy parents, was born in Lydda in Palestine in the third century and served in the Roman army. An imperial edict required that everyone suspected of Christianity should attend a pagan temple, sacrifice to the gods, blaspheme Christ and partake of food offered to idols. George, aged about 20, refused to do this and died a martyr. English interest in St George was greatly stimulated by the Crusades. In the reign of Edward III it was decreed that St George should be the nation's patron saint.

Evenley's church is part of the diocese of Peterborough and the ecclesiastical parish of Evenley in the benefice of Astwick Vale. The benefice is made up of the parishes of Aynho, Croughton, Evenley, Farthinghoe and Hinton-in-the-Hedges with Steane.

Vicars since 1945 have been
1942 James Walter Monks
1952 John Wilfred Hollies Bullock
1961 Gwilym Gaswallon Howell Phillips
1972 Douglas Gordon Catt (priest in charge)
1976 George James Green
1996 Peter Gompertz
2006 Gill Barker

Recent churchwardens have been
Madeline Furnivall and Carrie O'Regan
Jose Golding and Paul Bennett

As well as its services, the Church in Evenley has many other functions, in particular:-

The Welcome Pack
The Church provides a very helpful welcome package for newcomers to the village.

The package contains a mass of information including churches, schools, hospitals, medical and dental practices, bin collections and bus timetables. Also listed are plumbers, electricians, window cleaners, details about societies and activities centred on the Village Hall and how to contact relevant organisers. There is information about the Parish Council, the Residents Association and Neighbourhood Watch. Indeed anything a new resident needs to get started in the village.

The Choir and Organist
Nick Russell took over the Choir from Ron Hartnell at the end of 1986. He subsequently added the Shelswell Group Choir and also singers from Aynho, Croughton, Farthinghoe and Hinton. and they sang varied and interesting music. The Choir sang at Christmas and for special occasions such as weddings. Kevin O'Regan took over the Choir when Nick left the village and ran it for a year. John Oley was, and still is, the organist.

Bellringing
The bells, which were in a very bad state, were restored by Peter Fleckney and rehung in the ringing chamber in 1992 which was followed by a Thanksgiving service at which a quarter peal was rung. They were able to be restored as part of the Spire Appeal which raised £27,000 for replacing the shingled roof. Peter Fleckney has repaired and rehung 104 bells in his lifetime without any recompense! He worked on the bells of St. Martin in the Fields in the 1980's so we were lucky to have him restore our peal. Two of our five bells were forged in 1632 and one is a very special bell. Number 3 has an unidentified coat of arms on it, with the motto "honi soit qui mal y pense", the motto of the Order of the Garter, a bit of a puzzle! A number of villagers ring the bells which make a beautiful sound on a Sunday morning, at weddings and funerals.

The Clock
The Church Clock was restored with a donation in memory of Richard Franklin. Ian Chapple cleaned up the clock and restored it. An 'expert' had looked at it and pronounced that the clock would have to be removed and thoroughly overhauled and repaired which would cost a lot of money. Ian looked at it and decided he could do it in situ and worked on it with the help of Joe Glenham. It was back in working order in late 1999 and then the dial was restored later. It has been wound ever since, first by Peter Oxley and then by Paul Bennett, who still does it twice a week and has done for most of this century.

Sunday School
Madeline Furnivall took the Sunday School in the 1980's and also gave Bible Study classes at Evenley Hall with Ron Hartnell and Fiona Mason. Madeline gave up the Sunday School when she became a Church Warden which she was for many years.

The Sunday School took place in the Village Hall, run by various people throughout the years, including Carolyn Oley and Chris Cousins. Now all children in the Parish are welcomed at Aynho where the Benefice Sunday School takes place.

The village lunch
This takes place on the first Tuesday of each month and is open to all in the village. It is simple – soup and a sandwich – for a modest price. It was started

by Nick Russell shortly after Randall Hunter closed the Shop in 1989, when he left the village, in order to keep people in touch and has flourished ever since.

Holiday Club

This was started in the late 1990's as a Holiday Club for five to eleven year olds from all the five parishes in the Benefice. It happens during five consecutive days in August and is run by volunteers from the five parishes and a group of teenagers help. It is held at All Saints C of E Primary School in Croughton and up to 80 children usually attend.

Evenley Charities

Evenley Charities was started in 1780 by a gift of land to enable the income from it to be available for the poor of Evenley

The land is two fields on the far side of the Buckingham road opposite Bicester Hill. One field is for poor widows and the other is for the Church.

The trustees of the Charities, which continue to this day, include the Vicar and the Churchwardens of Evenley Parish Church.

THE POCKET PARK

History

Pocket Parks are open spaces providing free access to the countryside. They originated in Northamptonshire where they were first established in the early 1980s.

The land on which the Evenley Pocket Park was established had been allocated for stone pits in the village enclosure of 1780. The site is common land which was used for sheep grazing many years ago. In the years running up to the site becoming a Pocket Park it remained relatively unused and suffered from illicit dumping of rubbish, particularly after the sale of the Evenley Hall Estate in 1938. During the war it was used as an ammunition dump and some people can remember rabbiting there at some risk to themselves. At some stage it was probably known as the People's Park.

Establishing the Park

The site was established as a Pocket Park in 1989 and was set up by Tom Chester, who was an acknowledged expert on lichens and on wildlife, working in partnership with Northamptonshire County Council and South Northamptonshire County Council, who both provided a grant. He planted the roadside hedge, did the original plan of the Park, made the flora and fauna inventory and was the warden as well as producing a newsletter!

The Park is 1.6 acres in size, which is just over half the size of the Green and is owned by the Parish Council. It is now managed by the Evenley Pocket Park Group made up of a Parish Councillor, Merrick Loggin, whose business is just opposite the park and who is the warden, and people from the village. It is situated off Bicester Hill and is grassland with shrubs, thickets and mature trees. It also has a table and a number of benches.

Wildlife

The grassland contains two rare plants, the Dark Mullein and the Knapweed Broomrape.

The Dark Mullein is a semi evergreen biennial plant of the figwort family. It is clump forming with tall, branched, flower stems. These carry golden yellow flowers with a purple centre from June until September providing nectar and

The Pocket Park

pollen to bees. The seeds provide food for numerous seed-eating creatures.

The Knapweed Broomrape is a parasitic plant and lives off the Greater Knapweed which grows on lime soils to a height of about two feet. It has a yellowish stem, brown leaves and yellow/brown flowers in tall dense spikes from mid July to mid August. It is also host to the Marbled White butterfly.

The Marbled White is a rarity in this county as it is mainly located in the south west of England. However it can be seen here between mid June and mid August.

The Park is also visited by foxes, muntjac deer, grass snakes, small mammals and numerous species of birds.

Maintenance

Maintenance of the site is mainly done by annual grass cutting in late summer and composting. The scrubland is managed by creating clearings to encourage bluebells and the scrub is cut every five years to encourage the regeneration of the Blackthorn.

Usage

As well as being a small wildlife centre the Park is used for a variety of things including the Gardening Society's annual barbecue.

FOOTPATHS AND BRIDLEWAYS

There are at least ten footpaths and three bridleways in the Parish. Five of the footpaths start in the village and lead to Brackley, the Great Ouse, Juniper Hill, Astwick and the A43 just short of Elm Tree Farm respectively.

Footpaths and bridleways are technically "rights of way" over land owned by individuals and organisations. Northamptonshire County Council is legally responsible for those in Evenley working with our Footpath Warden, Michael Johnson, who took over the job in 1994. He liaises with the Council where any problems arise and walks all the footpaths in the Parish periodically.

The main responsibilities of N.C.C. are for the signage, gates and stiles, keeping the paths clear, which sometimes involves mowing and tarmacking. It also involves making sure that the landowner plays his part, particularly ensuring that crops do not obscure the paths.

Rights of way are protected by quite a lot of legislation and established practice over the years. One of the unexpected consequences of legislation is that where a dual carriageway, such as the A43 is built the right of way continues across the road. This leads to the somewhat bemusing sign which states "Beware pedestrians crossing". You might think that the pedestrians should be the ones to beware!

HOUSING DEVELOPMENTS

The expansion of Evenley

Evenley has only been able to develop from the primarily agricultural village of 1945 to its present size and population of about 600 through a number of housing developments and the infilling of available plots. In order to be able to do this there were extra services which needed to be in place. These were:-

Electricity

Electricity came to the village in 1932 - 1934 from the East Midlands Electric Light Company. Now everyone has a choice of suppliers.

Water

The expansion of the housing stock also depended on the arrival of mains water which came in the 1950s. Until then water for the village had come from the main wind-driven water-pump and a number of smaller hand pumps one of which was behind Dormer Row and another behind the row of houses on the North East side of the Green.

The main water-pump was as tall as the highest house in the village and was situated on the right hand side of what is now Church Leys, near the present day allotments, and fed a small reservoir to provide most of the water for Evenley. It was taken down as part of the development of Church Leys but before it went it very nearly removed someone's fingers. There was also another wind-driven water pump where the sewage farm is now.

A wind driven water pump

Street Lighting
Another factor in helping the increase in housing was the introduction of street lighting. The Parish Council, Chairman Stanley Fox, was given the go-ahead at the Annual Parish Meeting in March 1969. It was decided that:-

> "to preserve the character of the village there will be no lamp posts erected in the centre of the village. Lamps will be put on brackets attached to houses round the village green and to existing electricity posts."

Housing Developments
These developments came on fields previously part of the surrounding farms and in this order:-

Lawyers Close, on the left hand side of Broad Lane as you leave the village, was built in 1966 on what had been called Brandon Estate and previously a field called Lawyers Close. It consists of 30 houses and bungalows. The origin of this field name is not known.

Rudgeway was built in 1970-71 and is half way up School Lane on the left. It was built on Bone Hill, on what had originally been allotments. It comprises eight bungalows.

Church Leys was built in 1979 and is on part of a field of that name which also included the old Rectory Farm. The field had housed the village football pitch and cricket ground; it also had the tall water pump which served many of the houses in the village. The development comprises 22 houses and bungalows.

The origin of the word Leys is obscure but one opinion is that it refers to leylines which are believed to be invisible tracks or lines in the ground linking sacred places and natural magical sites. If the part of the area which remains a field is ever developed the inhabitants may be in for a few surprises!

Franklin's Yard was built on the site of the Park Farm barns in 1989 and consists of nine two storey houses. The development backs onto "The Moat", the origin of which is unknown. The development was renamed Franklin's Yard in 1999 in honour of Richard Franklin who had farmed there.

The future Franklin's Yard in about 1959

Spencer Close, comprising seven houses and a further three fronting Broad Lane of four or five bedrooms, was built in 2002 on the site of the allotments which had been owned by Cicely Spencer. Due to the efforts of the Parish Council and the Residents Association part of the site was retained for allotments for the use of the village.

Infilling

Infilling has also taken place in the village at various times. It started with the building of 11 Council houses in School Lane in 1947. The next infilling took place along Broad Lane, which in Bill Buggins's time had an avenue of Elms. Substantial detached houses were built and, most recently, three semi-detached houses in School Lane.

In total there are 246 houses in the Parish of Evenley giving an average occupation of about 2.4 people per house, about the national average.

AGRICULTURE

Agriculture has always been important to Evenley and was particularly so during and after the end of the war. Although there have been many changes in the last seventy years it still remains important, not just locally, but also nationally as it provides the base on which many other industries and services depend.

There have been, and still are, both livestock and arable farms in the Parish. The actual number of farms has declined through amalgamation but very little land has been lost by farming apart from some to housebuilding.

Changes in agriculture

The main trends which have affected all farming are well known and are the effects of mechanisation on employment, the introduction, and in many cases the rejection, of chemicals and the effects of regulation from London and Brussels.

On the upside, however, milk yields in cows have risen substantially, through better knowledge of animal husbandry and better use of feedstocks. In the past all milk was sold through the Milk Marketing Board and a price was set. Nowadays you have to find your buyer and fix a price (or more usually accept the price offered!)

Livestock

Fifty or so years ago many farms around Evenley were mixed with dairy, sheep, some pigs and arable. Many farms in the Parish had a few dairy cows and there were six with pedigree Jersey herds, although they were small. Now the only dairy herd is the Barnowl herd of Charles and Frances Reader with 85 cows and youngstock, established in 1970 and transferred to Evenley in 1984.

This herd at Cloisters Farm is one of the top herds in the country both for type and milk production. One of their brood cows, Barnowl Fanfare, is still the U.K. record holder for type with a 97% rating and has held many production and type trophies in her time. Several of her sons went to stud and some of her descendants are still in the herd and others overseas.

Charles is renowned as a national and international judge of cattle and is a

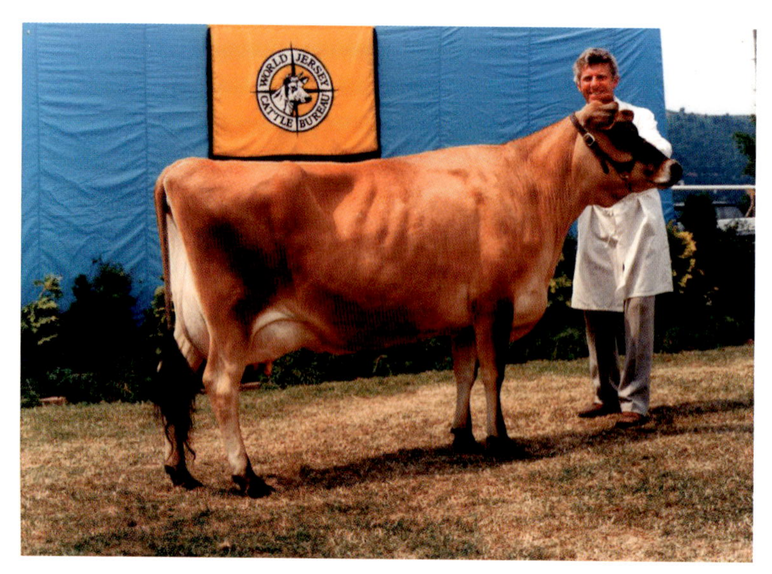

Barnowl Fanfare

past president of the Jersey Cattle Society. He often consults with the NFU and DEFRA on policies.

Arable

There are many farms around Evenley which specialise in arable. One such is Robert Hawes's at Bowling Green. Unusually he also has sheep which thrive on the limestone soil. His main crops are wheat, barley and oats. He is also experimenting with diversification and is growing peas in 2010. These crops are sold on contract to a merchant where he can either agree a price in advance or take the current price on delivery – a bit of a gamble!

He is in a scheme called ELS which means he is paid for low intensive farming with the minimum of fertilisers. He is also in a scheme where he sows ½ hectare of pollen and nectar plants to encourage insects. These schemes are to encourage more natural farming and benefit wildlife. Robert's neighbours say that he has the most wildlife on his farm of any of them.

THE NATIONAL CHILDREN'S HOME AND EVENLEY HALL

During the war the Hall was occupied initially by the East Yorks Yeomanry and their tanks were parked along the drive from the Lodge to the Hall.

It was then occupied by evacuees when the Yeomanry moved out. After the war was over it became a children's home in one form or another until 2001 when it was put up for sale and returned to private ownership.

Bill Clark's tenure

About 12 children who were unable to be cared for by their parents lived there to start with, being cared for by Bill Clark and some National Children's Home sisters. They had the Park to play in and used to swim in the river Ouse. They took part in Scouts and Girl Guides, country dancing and music and gave performances all over the country at NCH festivals. They attended local schools and played sports such as football and tennis, at which they were very good. The television cameras even covered a Christmas party at the Hall.

Mike Barlow takes over

In 1970 Bill Clark was promoted to become an N.C.H. area manager and Mike Barlow and his wife, Ceinwen, and their four children took over. They lived in the Lodge at the end of Evenley Hall Lime Tree drive.

The number of children, which had grown from the original 12 to a maximum of 57 in five family groups, was reduced to 30 in three family groups. Staff included married couples who both worked there.

Holidays

Summer holidays were organised in groups at the seaside or caravan parks, youth hostels etc. at home or even France. One year on returning from France in heavy snow they drove along the A34 to Oxford when most vehicles couldn't get through. The AA could not believe that they had made it but they had strong lads who cleared the path or pushed from time to time! The next day the Evenley Hall drive was blocked for several days.

The children were well educated at school and in outdoor activities such as camping and fishing and taught to help others. They loved the freedom of the grounds and one lad slept all night up a tree! Madeline Furnival and her husband Gordon moved to Evenley Hall to help look after the children.

When the end of schooling came and they returned to their home areas it was sometimes difficult to adjust to an ordinary life style. With this difficulty the Social Services decided to cease sending children to the Hall in the early 1980's.

Children with learning difficulties

However in 1984 the Hall became a home for young people with learning difficulties. Seven students started there following the Evenley Hall Community Project and taking part in a "Training for Life" programme with their parents' backing. Staff retrained and students were encouraged to become as independent as possible. By 1997 the students were doing 'out work' and attending evening classes in Brackley and day courses at Banbury College. They used public transport as well as the two minibuses. These activities and holidays were all geared to learning independence.

There were volunteers - Friends of Evenley Hall - who helped at the Hall and were a tremendous asset.

Change of Management

In 1997 the Shaftesbury Society took over from the N.C.H. - Action for Children - because the age range was moving out of N.C.H. charitable status. There was a full range of day training in the Hall and the grounds including basic education with computers, house management, catering, craft work and gardening activities in the grounds.

Sale of the Hall

There was also a plan for the Hall to be sold in five years' time and the income put back into child care. So in 2001 the residents moved into six houses in Brackley.

The Hall is now owned and lived in by Chris and Emma Wightman and after 3 years of planning discussions with South Northants planning department, and significant local support (a key to the application's success) a scheme of alteration and almost total restoration was agreed.

Today the Hall has been largely returned to its original Georgian splendour, while the magnificent Victorian staircase has been restored in such a way that the juxtaposition of architectural styles blend rather than grate.

The restoration of the Hall being now complete, the formerly grand gardens and parkland are being replanted to their former glory. Already the lakes, lost at the end of the 19th century, are back, many trees have been planted in the Park and the main garden has been cleared to the point where the original structure can now be seen. Finally the cricket pitch, once used by the village, is to be resurrected, and this handsome, warm and welcoming building in its beautiful setting has now been returned, hopefully forever, to private family use.

The back of Evenley Hall as it is today

CLUBS, SOCIETIES AND ORGANISATIONS

The Evenley Women's Institute, or W.I. as it is more usually called, was founded in 1948 by Cicely Spencer, Ivy Pratt, Rene Seaton, Olive Westlake, Elizabeth Syson and others. They used to meet in the Institute Room, or Working Mens Club, which is now the Village Shop.

The national W. I.

The W.I. was formed in 1915 to revitalise rural communities and encourage women to produce more food during the First World War.

Now it provides women with educational opportunities, chances to build new skills and to take part in a variety of activities and campaign on issues that matter in their community. It is, of course, a way of meeting people and building friendships.They run Denford College near Abingdon where members of the W.I. can attend courses on a large variety of subjects from politics to craft making.

It is funded by annual subscriptions, grants, donations and sponsorship and a trading arm, W.I. Enterprises.

The Emblem, embroidered by Olive Westlake

The Evenley W.I.

The members of the Evenley W.I. on its 40th anniversary in 1988 were

Barbara Bailey
Joyce Bailey
Evelyn Barber
Ceinwen Barlow
Molly Bright
Maureen Brinkworth
Margo Buttery
Corsie Chester
Ruth Cooper
Jane Duty
Barbara Evans
Molly Fox
Madeline Furnivall
Joan Grundy
Joyce Hall
Rita Hartnell
Gina Harvey
Margaret Herbert
Kittie Jefferies
June Johnson
Brenda King
Inga Latheron
Kath Lennard
Thelma Morgan
Carrie O'Regan
Janet Pearce
Ivy Pratt
Vi Purves
Irene Seaton
Jane Snell
Maureen Socota
Kath Taylor
Jan Tibble
Molly Trussell
Pat Ure
Doris Walduck
Eleanor Watson
Olive Westlake
Vi Whetter
Jessie Wildes

In 2010 it is still a thriving organisation, although they do not have as many members as they did in the past. This is due to a change in lifestyle. Before there was television people made their own entertainment. It was a source of friendship and a way of meeting people. People also worked nearer home and less women went out to work. Now more often than not husband and wife go out to work and have less time in the evening for joining clubs. Also the younger members of the village with children do not find it easy to go out in the evening. This is very much a problem nationwide.

Activities

Some of the activities which the W.I. have put on in the past include plays by their Choir and Drama Group, Fashion Shows, Flower Arranging, Cake decoration – icing a cake and making sugar flowers - Needlework and many more. They have lectures and demonstrations and also do a great deal for charity. They entertained the people from the Cheshire Homes giving them a cooked lunch, tea and taking them for a walk round the Green. Also they have produced teas for the open days of the Rare Breeds – and run out of cakes, but a member produced some from her freezer to save the day! They have done teas for the fetes on the Green and the Millennium celebrations when they gave a sundial to the village which has been put on the Village Hall.

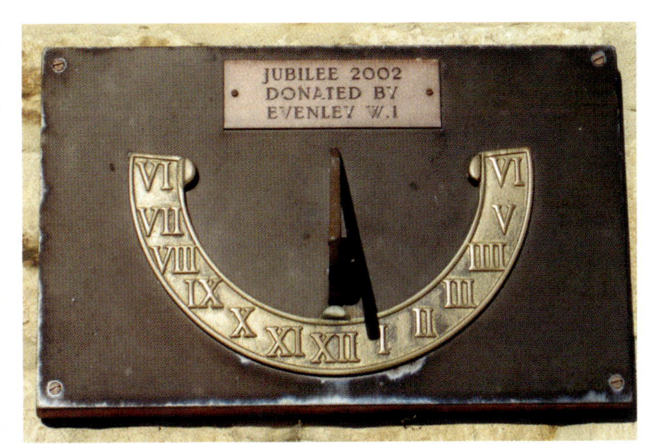

The sundial

They have collected clothes etc. and packed them in boxes for Slovenia. They planted bulbs on the verges at the beginning of Broad Lane. They have a working party, started by Molly Bright, which meets once a month and makes sweaters, wheelchair and cot blankets and baby clothes for deprived mothers and children in Northampton; also for Romania and Oxfam. They held competitions both for their members and at the Brackley Carnival where they won 2nd place in 1988

For their members they arrange mystery tours and weekends away. They remember their members' birthdays and anniversaries and their own Ruby, Golden and Diamond anniversaries, the latter being celebrated in 2008

Their oldest member, VI Purves, is over 90 and she swam every week until recently!

The celebratory cake

The national AGM

The W.I. have their AGM in the Albert Hall and one member from each area attends. Evenley has been represented several times.

The Evenley Film Club was set up in late 2002 by Brian Howells after a suggestion from Ian Mackway (Chairman of the Village Hall Committee at that stage) that residents of the village would welcome being able to see films in the Hall as opposed to having to drive to local cinemas. The first film was shown in February 2003 (Fried green tomatoes at the Whistle Stop Cafe), with the DVD player loaned by Brian and a slide projector and screen borrowed from a local business, RAPS UK. Brian, with the support of Ian, Mark Gibb as Treasurer and a small committee of members, ran the club until 2008, showing films roughly once every six weeks.

The re-launch

The film club was re-launched in 2009 by the Committee which currently comprises seven people (Alison Atkins, Mark Gibb, Ian Mackway, Brian and Heather Howells and John & Caroline Gilbart). The film club purchased sound and projection equipment with some financial support from the Co-op local supermarket and the Village Hall Committee. The South Northants Arts Council Scheme "Centre Screen Northamptonshire", part of the Rural Cinema Network, provides the club with films at affordable rates, and the Committee selects the films and shares overall responsibility for running the club. Films are now shown every four to six weeks.

The Bridge Club is one of the oldest Clubs in the village, apart from the Cricket Club. It was founded in 1977 by Jessie Wildes, Stephanie Leper, Joan

Gurr and one other. They still have two original members playing, Rosalind May, President, and Roy Hine. The Club started with ten tables and at its height reached sixteen tables. Jessie was the leading light insisting that pots of tea, savouries and magnificent cakes were served by two stewards who also put out the cards and oversaw the proceedings. They used to have weekends away in Sidmouth organised by Jessie. She resigned in 1993 and a formal Committee was then created with a constitution. They had their 20th anniversary in 1997 at the Crown Hotel, Brackley.

Jose Golding is the present Chairman and Social Secretary. They have about 6 tables and play for 1p a point, which is what they have always played for so the real value of their wins or losses has decreased substantially over the last thirty years!

The Flower Club is part of Brackley Flower Club. They meet on the first Tuesday of every month. It is open to residents of Evenley and Brackley. They have National Demonstrators to come and lecture, competitions, workshops and trips to gardens. They helped arrange the flower festival in the Church in 2009 and Denise Stevens does flower arrangements for weddings and services throughout the year with the help of Janet Cropley.

The Gardening Society was founded over thirty years ago and is now part of the village's DNA. One of the society's founder members, Ted Cox, raised almost all the bedding plants sold at the annual plant sale in his own Broad Lane garden and greenhouse. Ted also organised the society's seed order scheme which still enables members to secure a sizeable discount on their orders made through the society. Other early stalwarts of the society include former Chairman, Geoff Whetter, and Secretary, Jack Chapman.

Monthly meetings

In its early days the society used to hold annual flower and vegetable shows but these were discontinued due to a lack of support. However the society has grown stronger in other ways and regularly attracts around fifty of its members including many from Brackley and most of our surrounding villages to its popular monthly meetings which are addressed by a variety of specialist visiting speakers. Topics covered at meetings range from worm farming to plant hunting in South Africa with other evenings devoted to particular plant species. There's always the opportunity to meet the speakers over a cup of tea or coffee after the talk. On Tuesday evenings in June, July and August members visit delightful local gardens including those which are not normally open to the public.

Coach excursions

Ken and Betty Ames, sadly no longer with us, pioneered the coach excursion tradition. They carried out numerous forays to find really interesting destinations including the gardens of the royal residence at Highgrove and arranged the charter of a Thames cruiser to visit the Saville Gardens at Windsor. When Ted Cox left the village Ken took over his seed ordering duties.

The society's membership card has always been the passport to obtaining a discount at local nurseries and, in former years, such savings would easily cover the cost of the annual membership subscription. Now many garden centres and nurseries have established their own discount schemes but there are still several local nurseries willing to grant a discount on members' purchases.

Other activities

Other society activities highlighted in the newsletter include a summer barbeque on Evenley's Pocket Park and a party at Christmas when the Society welcome the village carol singers. Past projects have included the production and sale of a calendar comprising photographs of Evenley village scenes taken at various times during the year. The annual plant sale in the Village Hall goes from strength to strength albeit with plants and shrubs sourced from local nurseries rather than being grown in the village itself. Cliff and Brenda Payne now run the society's seed order scheme.

The society is always happy to recruit new members especially those who are interested in discovering more about gardens and gardening. Meetings are in Evenley Village Hall on the third Tuesday of the month.

The Youth Club was started 12–13 years ago by Linda Scaysbrook. Over the years, due to an increase in numbers, Denise Stevens and volunteers have assisted Linda. It is open to children from 11–16 years old living in the Parish of Evenley. They meet every Friday during term time from 7.30–9.30 pm in the village hall. The activities include table tennis, snooker, table football, air hockey, a games console with a wii, television, board and card games, a Disco several times a year and skate boarding. In summer they also play on the Green. It is very popular in the village. Brackley children used to come, but now they have a youth club twice a week in Brackley as Linda brought pressure to bear on the Council advising them of the considerable need for a youth club in Brackley.

CLIMATE

The country's climate has changed somewhat over these years, whether man made or due to other factors, and so has Evenley's. The main difference has been the absence, until recently, of cold winters with heavy snow; however the village is still something of a "frost pocket" because it is in a slight hollow.

In the past there has been skating and ice hockey on at least one of the four ponds which are on either side of the Mixbury road. There has also been tobogganing on the slopes around the village.

The village has been cut off, but not too seriously, particularly in the winters of 1946/7, 1956/7, 1986/87, 2009 and 2010.

The Parish Council has an appointed snow warden who, sensibly, lives outside the village.

The Snows of 2009 and 2010

Both these recent years have had unusual snowfalls and subsequent dislocation with 2009 having the most severe effects and 2010 the colder and longer lasting.

In 2009 we had the "Great Evenley Whiteout" when the bad weather started on Sunday 1st February. On Monday the whole of London shut down; there was no bus service whatsoever and the underground service was very limited.

Chiltern Railways battled on bravely but any further travelling had to be done on foot. Some airports were closed, Heathrow and Gatwick for the best part of a day and local airports in the Midlands for longer.

Evenley was not badly affected until the Wednesday night when the snow started falling in earnest and continued through Thursday. Temperatures barely rose above freezing so Thursday, Friday and most of Saturday were a complete white-out. The village was cut off and schools shut; cars became buried under six inches of snow and the post didn't arrive. Brackley shops ran out of fresh fruit and vegetables but the Evenley shop managed to keep supplied and stay open although trips to the Cash 'n Carry had to be postponed.

The children made the most of their surprise freedom. From somewhere - probably the dark corners of sheds – as well as the Village Shop, toboggans and sledges appeared. Some imaginative snowmen appeared on the Village Green. One lucky dog, rather than battle with the deep snow and icy paths, travelled round the village sitting regally on a sled.

The igloo

Most impressive of all an enormous "des.res." igloo was built on the Green, leading to the following exchange of e-mails:-

"There is an enormous igloo on the Green (and mark my words – NO PLANNING PERMISSION WAS GIVEN)!!!!!!"

"We very much enjoyed your comment about the igloo. May we use it in Characters?"

"Why not – after all said and done most buildings these days need planning permission – the number of rooms comes into question and I feel that the entrance way is far too large and is completely out of character with the streetscene. Detached house – cottage, bungalow or igloo are all subject to planning rules!!!!"

"and furthermore as the igloo is in a Conservation Area any application for retrospective planning permission should be frozen"

Travel

During the early stages of the blizzards nearly all roads were gritted but quite soon supplies were exhausted and what was left was reserved for the main roads. Brackley did not get treated and the hill became an ice rink. Cars were abandoned throughout the town.

Normal service was resumed after a week but thick banks of snow still remained two weeks later.

Seasons as seen in Evenley

FLORA AND FAUNA

As the village is surrounded by farmland it is not surprising that there is a fair amount of "infilling" by various horticultural and wildlife "activists", The flora, apart from the weeds, are almost exclusively introduced by humans, although the fauna come on their own accord.

Flora

Anyone driving into Evenley, seeing the Green with its magnificent trees or walking around the roads and the housing enclaves, will realise that the village is undoubtedly a village of gardens and gardeners. Not surprisingly, the village has a flourishing Garden Society and at least three qualified Landscape Gardeners.

Gardens

In addition there are two magnificent gardens which are open to the public under the National Gardens Scheme. These are

Janet and Bob Cropley's garden at Hill Grounds.

Their house was originally a bothy and cowsheds for Evenley Hall. The walled garden at the Hall provided insufficient space so a further 1½ acres was taken in hand during the 19th century, behind a yew hedge, the annual cuttings of which have been sent to a company which makes drugs for treating cancer.

The new area has been lovingly cultivated, giving a south facing slope with wonderful soil and shelter on the north and east. It was the site which attracted Bob and Janet as long ago as 1983 and they hardly bothered to enter the house and made an offer immediately!

The garden's evolution

Like most gardens it evolved as more time became available and new (gardening!) fancies took them forward. There are now four pergolas, all with different structures to give height, many fine trees and shrubs, with an emphasis on winter flowering, like viburnums and cherries, some inherited at the time of the purchase. As the soil is light it is good for bulbs, particularly those which come from southern Europe like crocus, iris and tulip which need sharp drainage and a good summer baking! Other fancies are for ornamental onions and foxgloves – there are many different kinds of the latter, some perennial and all promiscuous, so interbreeding produces some lovely hybrids.

The Millenium Arborette

To celebrate the millennium Janet and Bob took in a corner of their arable field and created a native shelter belt of mixed planting to make an "Arborette" for a few select forest trees, weeping limes, red oak and golden ash. They also added large shrubs like cotoneasters, elders and buddlias which cope with conditions in grass. Mowing is minimal and strips have been planted with indigenous flora. As nature has a way of pushing open any door left ajar they now have some naturalised wildings like St John's Wort and scabious and are honoured by a bee orchid as well as seeing an improvement in the insect life.

Because the site is sheltered they are able to grow a range of plants usually too tender for Central Britain although the calciferous nature of the soil does not allow for camellias, rhododendrons, azaleas and the like. These go into lime free soil in pots in the shade.

Entry to the Garden

As the garden matured, people expressed an interest in seeing it so they opened for the National Gardens Scheme and have an engraved trowel to celebrate 21 years of opening! Entrance is year long, by appointment, both for groups and individuals.

Evenley Wood Garden

The other amazing garden in the Parish, situated off the Mixbury road, is of course, the 60 acre Evenley Wood. The wood was bought by Timmy Whiteley from Lance Harman in 1975 and what was then a wood has now been turned into a wonderful garden within the wood.

You can stroll through these 60 acres armed with a plan of the garden and helped by signs to return you to the entrance if you get lost. You will, depending on the season, see a rich variety of trees and plants flanking the many rides through the wood and also see the stream which flows through the middle of the wood with its pond.

Allium-pilosum

Eucalyptus niphophila

Iris Dutch Bronze

Lychnis Hill Grounds

Some of the many plants in Janet and Bob's garden

Rhododendrons, azaleas and camellias

Since buying the wood Timmy, with his wife, Jane, has developed the already existing collection of rhododendrons, azaleas and camellias, all occupying a band of acid soil which is quite unusual in this calciferous area.

Their two hundred or so magnolias are also magnificent in the spring but rather touchier with regard to soil. Timmy has been running trial beds for the Royal Horticultural Society to test their resilience to alkalinity before releasing them to their appropriate place in the wood.

Trees and Shrubs

There is also a range of trees, both the well established and the more recently planted, which includes acers, ash, horse chestnuts, limes, oaks, walnuts and many more. A particular speciality is the Evenley Gold Oak, one of five plants developed in Evenley. As well as giving shade to the rhododendrons and azaleas, which are undertree plants, many of these trees give glorious autumn colour which can also be seen from quite a distance.

Bulbs and summer flowering plants

Not content with this Timmy and Jane have created an extensive collection of woodland bulbs. Chionodoxas, crocus, snowdrops, cyclamen, daffodils and narcissi all flower within their seasons.

But even more follows later in the year with lilies, roses, clematis and other climbers, the largest collection of euonymus in Europe, a giant rhubarb over ten feet tall and many other summer flowering plants.

Fauna

They have also made their contribution to the fauna of the Parish by creating habitat for over 20 species of butterflies, an amazing 300 moths, over 80 birds, including guinea fowl and far too many insects to count!

And if that isn't enough there is a delightful cafe near the entrance which sells tea, coffee and excellent cakes, some of which are rumoured to come from the Village Shop.

Entry to the Garden

All this information and much more can be found on the website at www.evenleywoodgarden.co.uk

Evenley Wood Garden is open to the public, and for groups by appointment, most weekends in the Spring, Summer and Autumn for a modest entrance fee.

Quercus rubra aurium

Primula japonica

Viburnum

Paeony

Some of the many plants in Evenley Wood Garden

FAUNA

The fauna in the village fall naturally into three categories; birds, butterflies and animals.

Birds

Janet Cropley carries out a weekly survey for the British Trust for Ornithology covering birds seen in the Cropley's garden. This survey, nationally, is turning up a raft of hitherto unknown data about our common birds and the importance of gardens in bird ecology.

We regularly have visits from raptors, particularly kestrels, buzzards and sparrowhawks and have resident tawny owls. Other rare visitors are siskins, bramblings and gold crests. thrushes, robins, blackbirds, wrens and the five types of tit are present in good numbers. However the survey has highlighted a decline in spotted flycatchers, willow tits and starlings.

Down in the village there are numerous sightings of swallows, housemartins, tits, wrens, pigeons, songthrushes, sparrows, wagtails, blackbirds, chaffinches, fieldfares, woodpeckers, pheasants and even a red kite

The sparrowhawk

There was also a sparrowhawk which crashed into a conservatory window in pursuit of a fledgling blackbird. The sparrowhawk died and the blackbird survived after treatment by Ann Otterli.

Butterflies

As well as the substantial range of butterflies seen in Evenley Wood the following have been seen in the village itself

Large and Small Whites
Brimstone
Peacock
Burnet moth
Orange tip
Painted Lady
Meadow Brown
Comma
Small tortoiseshell
Common Blue
Red Admiral

These are just a few of the 57 varieties of butterfly seen in Britain

Some local butterflies: Red Admiral, Brimstone, Orange Tip and Painted Lady

Animals

The fauna which live or visit the village and its environs are quite varied with the inevitable foxes, rabbits, badgers and squirrels but also roe and fallow deer and muntjack, even seen in the garden of a house on the Green, happily eating its way through the owner's lovingly grown vegetables.

Less delightful are the adders and grass snakes seen in the pond of a garden in a house in Franklin's Yard.

Finally we must not forget the bats which glide almost silently around the village in the gloaming on a summer evening.

THE PARISH COUNCIL

Parish Councils were first formed by the Local Government Act of 1894. They are the first tier of Local Government providing a range of services at village or town level. Before that date ecclesiastical parishes had the responsibility for the relevant services.

Evenley's Parish Council became of increasing significance as the village expanded with new housing from the early 1960s.

Membership

The Evenley Council consists of a maximum of seven elected members with power to co-opt between elections. Elections take place every four years with an election in 2011. As well as the elected members there is a Parish Clerk and there are also four wardens appointed by the Council covering Trees, Footpaths, the Pocket Park and Snow. Finally there is a Highways representative and a Village Correspondent.

In 1999 Keith Cousins became Chairman and Mike Bosher Vice Chairman.

Previous Chairmen of the Council have included
Leonard Warren
Stanley Fox
Lance Harman
Cicely Spencer
Nigel Fox

and the most recent Parish Clerks have been
Sue Mullarkey
David Bush
Trish Mackway
Joyce Stevens

The Parish Council in session

Services

The Parish Council provides a wide range of services to the Parish some of which are regular items and others which are "one offs."

Its meetings are open for everyone to attend and normally take place every other month. They start with a ten minute period in which members of the village can raise issues they want discussed or resolved. There is an Annual General Meeting every year and the minutes of the monthly and annual meeting are displayed on the notice board inside the Village Hall.

Newsletter

The Parish Council's newsletter, which is published every other month and delivered to every home, contains items of interest to residents including news of forthcoming events and village activities.

Recent involvements

The recent problems which the Council has had to deal with are, first, the proposal to build a large number of houses on the allotment site, now Spencer Close. Working with the Residents Association, the number was substantially reduced and part of the site was preserved for allotments for the village, which had not been included in the original planning application.

Secondly the Council played a major part in getting the road crossing at the top of Broad Lane converted to a roundabout after several near misses ending with a fatal accident.

The other recent challenge has been the proposal for planning permission for a mast to measure wind speeds with the possibility of a wind turbine being erected close to the village. A village meeting was held under the auspices of the Residents Association. The Parish Council objected to the application and the proposal was subsequently rejected.

Other initiatives

The council has, naturally, been involved in or responsible for a number of other important initiatives recently, including:-

Refurbishing of the War Memorial,

Resolving the sewage problem in Puddleduck,

Replacing trees on the Green after the loss of four Chestnuts,

Replacing street lights around the village,

New road priorities at the Village Hall,

Providing furniture for the Pocket Park

Setting up Speedwatch jointly with the Residents Association

THE RESIDENTS ASSOCIATION AND NEIGHBOURHOOD WATCH

The Residents Association was formed in 2002, initially to reduce, successfully, the housing density on the proposed development of Spencer Close. This allowed part of the land to be retained for allotments.

The suggestion for an Association came from Ken Ames, a member of the Parish Council and was quickly taken up by various residents who called a village meeting at which a Committee and Constitution were approved. It is one of the few Residents Associations in South Northamptonshire.

Since then the Association has moved on to many other projects including assimilating the overall responsibility for Neighbourhood Watch and working jointly with the Parish Council on the problems of speeding in the village

Objectives

Its objectives are to work with the Parish Council in order to:-

- Improve the quality of life of village residents by developing local facilities.
- Protect the rural heritage of our village.
- Develop a sense of community by supporting and encouraging participation in community events.

Recent projects

Creating a subcommittee, jointly with the Parish Council, to review issues concerning road safety in the village.

Taking over responsibility for Neighbourhood Watch in the village.

Organising, presenting facts and Chairing a meeting to discuss the planning application for a wind turbine on Bicester Hill. The objective was for the proposal to receive a fair hearing and for those in favour and against to be able to put informed views to South Northants Council. The meeting attracted over 100 people.

Creating a village website to include information about the village and details of all village activities which want to be represented with links to related village sites such as the Shop, the Red Lion and the Cricket Club.

Donating to the fund for the restoration of the War Memorial.

Donating to and helping with the project to plant four new trees around the Green and planting daffodils under the auspices of the Gardening Society.

Publishing "Aspects of Evenley" in November 2002; the story of our village from pre Roman times to the Second World War.

Publishing "Tales of Evenley" in November 2005; the memoires of Cicely Spencer and Bill Buggins of the life and changes in our village in the 20th century.

Publishing "Characters of Evenley" about the remarkable characters who live and have lived in Evenley and make the village and its organisations what it is today.

Providing support for the village shop during the handover and subsequently helping with the marketing of it and the Post Office through leaflets and circulars.

Producing the Village Postcard and Christmas card.

Continuing to work with the Parish Council to find a suitable place to set up a play area for the young children of Evenley.

Chairmen
The first Chairman was Jim Brophy, followed by Chris Chippendale, Richard Darby, Andrew Bullock, Lyn Pyatt and Kay Baul.

Membership
Membership is open to everyone in the Parish for a nominal payment. The committee of about ten members hold meetings bimonthly.

The ERA in committee

An Annual General Meeting is held each year in the Spring.

The Association has had interesting speakers, including

Chris and Emma Wightman, owners of Evenley Hall.

Jean Morgan, Chief Executive of South Northants Council.

Lady Juliet Townsend, Lord Lieutenant of Northamptonshire.

Sandra Walker and Hayley Hammond talking about the Shop and the Red Lion.

Lord Boswell, retiring M.P. for the Constituency and Steve Hogarth, vocalist with the British Rock band, Marillion

The Association's objective remains to work with the Parish Council for the benefit of the people of Evenley.

CHARACTERS AND FAMILIES PAST AND PRESENT

There have been many Characters and Families who have contributed to the development of Evenley over the last seventy years. Some of them are included here and some elsewhere in the text. Sadly we have no record for those from the more distant past, but without all their efforts and dedication the village would not be the delightful place it is now.

Ken and Betty Ames

Evenley would have been very much the poorer had Ken and Betty not come to live here. They both, in their own ways, contributed a great deal to the village.

Ken and Betty Ames

Ken's life before Evenley

Ken lived in England until the age of twelve when his family moved to India. He went to boarding school there and later in England.

During the war he was in the Royal Engineers and posted to the Gulf. His regiment built a military supply road from the Gulf to the Russian border to assist the Russians. After the war his Corps then had to destroy the same road as Russia had changed from being an ally to a cold war enemy.

He remained in the army in India after the war and during the Muslim Hindu Civil War and in 1947 at the time of the establishment of Pakistan his regiment had to clear thousands of corpses from the streets. He never forgot this experience.

Ken worked in Lahore when he came out of the army and met Betty on one of his visits to England in 1964. They married and stayed in the Indian sub continent for twenty six years.

In 1964 they returned to England although he travelled to Africa in his job working for Coles Cranes. They moved to Evenley in the 1980's.

Betty's early life

Betty also had an interesting time before she met Ken. She was Dutch, born in Indonesia, moved to Egypt, Palestine and Holland with her family. She saw the first aeroplane built by Fokker in 1933.

In 1940 her family took the last ship to Indonesia the day before the Germans occupied Holland. They then had to go swiftly to Sidney due to the threat of Japanese invasion and then on to San Francisco for the same reason.

She worked as PA to the Dutch Commercial Attache, Private Secretary to the head of the Dutch Air Force and then went to university in Melbourne and obtained a BA and then an MA. All this before she met Ken!

Ken and Betty move to Evenley

In the 1980's Ken and Betty bought a house in Evenley and soon after came retirement with the opportunity to acquire new interests and friends.

Throughout his life in Evenley Ken dedicated himself to the well-being of the village and it is safe to say that he made a major contribution to most projects that have enhanced our life here. The most visible evidence of his contribution is the Village Hall where he was a key member of the team responsible for its refurbishment and its enlargement, keeping an eye on it and doing running repairs if necessary.

Parish councillor

As a parish councillor Ken invested boundless enthusiasm and dedication into activities which can sometimes be thankless. There was always the satisfaction of knowing that, if Ken committed himself to a task, it would be carried out and done well.

The Gardening Society

As President of the Evenley Gardening Society Ken's organisation of the coach excursions, two or three times a year, was legendary. Whereas before Ken's time it was difficult to arrange a viable trip, when Ken took over the organisation of trips on occasions a 78 seat luxury double decker coach would be filled and a waiting list would sometimes be necessary. On the day itself he would always have assembled a selection of facts and figures to make the day that bit more enjoyable. Over the years Ken and Betty drove thousands of miles visiting potential destinations including boatyards, garden centres and stately homes, sampling the cuisine and ensuring that the washrooms were adequate for a large coach party. The itinerary for each trip was meticulously planned with calls on coach companies to assess their vehicles and to ensure that each element of the excursion dovetailed with the next.

Attention to detail

Ken's fantastic attention to detail was also evident in his management of the society's seed order activities where he secured business in excess of £1000 per year thus gaining large discounts from the suppliers to enable members to benefit from lower prices. Amongst Ken's contributions to the society's annual plant sale was a trawl round the district's supermarkets from which he collected around sixty discarded cardboard boxes each year to enable customers to take their purchases safe home

Other contributions

Yet another of Ken's village activities has been the Neighbourhood Watch scheme whose success can be measured by the very low level of crime in the village.

He also suggested the formation of the Evenley Residents Association, originally to fight the development on the allotments, but also, as he pointed out, to work for the good of the village.

Both he and Betty loved their garden and all the animals and birds which visited. They were wonderful neighbours and friends to many in the village.

Ken and Betty made an enormous contribution to making Evenley what it is today.

There is an inscription on one of the benches on the Green which reads:-

"In memory of Ken Ames who contributed so much to our
village community 1924-2005"

"We also remember his devoted wife Betty 1921-2007.
A kind and gracious lady".

Dick and Mollie Bright

The Brights moved to Evenley in about 1960 from London, and lived in Gulliver's cottage. Dick had held a senior position in Public Relations with the BBC, at a time when Public Relations were unheard of.

Dick was in the Navy during the war, partly in Alexandria, and may also have worked at Bletchley Park on code-breaking, but as those who worked there were sworn to secrecy and kept to it, we will probably never know.

Dick's combination of urbane charm, friendliness and love of the village naturally led him to be known as "the Womble of Evenley" for his habit of worrying about everything, including picking up rubbish. He was a very suitable Clerk to the Parish Council where his somewhat forthright manner had its impact at a very formative time for the Council. He was known as "Flags" to his Chairman, Leonard Warren, as they had both been in the Navy.

Dick Bright looking quizzical

He was highly literate - as became a BBC veteran – and among other things he helped Bill Buggins with the drafting of his memoir recording his recollections of life in Evenley in the 20th century. He also helped a young man who had written a short history of Mediaeval Northamptonshire to be interviewed by Radio Northampton following which it was accepted into the County archive.

Mollie was a great support to Dick and a delightful person who was much liked in the village. She was a niece of Clement Attlee, Prime Minister from 1945-51. She was reputed never to drive at more than 15 miles an hour. Dick died in 1985 and Mollie a few years later.

Bill and Mattie Buggins

Bill Buggins was the first historian of Evenley and one of its most remarkable Characters.

Without his memories published in "Tales of Evenley" we would not have such a rich background to draw on both for so many of the things which happened in Evenley in the 20th century and for the details of the agriculture on which the village depended for so long. That publication told us a lot about Evenley. Hopefully this entry will tell more about Bill himself and about his wife, Mattie

Bill's grandfather settled in Evenley in about 1845-50 and lived at No. 5

Dormer Row. Bill was born in Evenley in 1902 and also lived most of his life at No. 5 Dormer Row, having started married life with Mattie in a cottage at Rectory Farm where she worked.

"Buggins Row"

Over time he bought all but one of the cottages making up Dormer Row for £500 each (roughly £25,000 in today's money) from a Mr. Turvey who had bought them in the sale of the Evenley Hall Estate in 1938. (The remaining cottage was owned by Cicely Spencer who installed her nanny there so that she did not have to see the washing!)

Indeed Dormer Row might, in those days, have been more appropriately named "Buggins Row", with so much of it in Buggins' hands. Rumour has it that the Buggins were the prime movers in installing front doors opening onto the Green in defiance of the wishes of the Squire who felt that "servants" (i.e. the wives of farm labourers) should face the rear so that she did not have to see them gossiping or feeding their babies!

Family

Bill lived there with Mattie after they left Rectory Farm until he died in 1976. His brother, Harry, who served in the R A F and then worked in Brackley was a bachelor and lived at no. 6. Bill's son Leslie lived at no. 5 until 2008. Leslie's older brother Tommy married but did not have any children and lived in Middleton Cheney. Bill and Mattie also fostered two adopted boys, Norman & Charlie.

Interests and studies

Bill worked in agriculture and subsequently at the RAF Croughton Base. He also had a great memory and a lively and meticulous interest in all that went on in Evenley and beyond. Bill had many memories of Evenley past, particularly the four ponds which had existed; spinney pond, fish pool, middle pond and new pond. He also recalled the breaking up of the four great estates in the area, Aynho, Shelswell, Mixbury and, of course, Evenley Hall estate.

Apart from his booklet on Evenley, now one of the two memoirs in "Tales of Evenley", he was also responsible for recording at least two other studies about those times.

Dialects

One was his essay on the dialects that existed in the area before the First World War with a report on the reasons for the post war decline in the dialect. This was an extensive study which also included the old fashioned names for the towns and villages; thus Rackley for Brackley, Inton for Hinton, Imley for

Evenley and so on. It also included the special language which was used to communicate with horses.

His essay identified the way in which dialects had changed, first as a result of the able bodied farm workers going to the war and taking their dialects with them. They were replaced by men from other parts of the country with their own dialects. Then in the period between the wars the effect of greater mobility of the population through improved means of travel meant that the old accents began to disappear or become amalgamated.

Old field names

Bill's other important work was on the old field names which he meticulously recorded on a special map.

With some like Conygra and Hootitty even Bill did not know the reason for their names but others have been faithfully recorded and are listed elsewhere in this book.

Special constable

Bill, and his father and grandfather before him were Special Constables in the Police Force. Bill became a "Special" in 1938, and was the first volunteer from Evenley for war work. He did this along with all his farming duties at Rectory Farm and afterwards at the RAF Croughton Base. He and his father kept a firm eye on all aspects of the village. He said "my father worked at one end of the village and I worked at the other. Between us we didn't miss a thing!" One suspects between them they dispensed justice in the old fashioned way and that no one was the worse for it.

Bill was awarded the Special Constabulary Long Service medal and in 1969 he was awarded a bar to the medal for an additional 10 years service.

A Special Constabulary Long Service Medal

Village activities

Right up to the end of his life Bill took a full and active interest in village goings on. These included the village's traditional annual Olde Tyme Music Hall, held in the Village Hall. Under the urbane stewardship of the BBC's Dick Bright as Master of Ceremonies, everyone did their turn and great fun was had by all. It was customary for Bill to sing a Victorian ballad in his own special way. On one occasion Bill was in full flow with his unique rendering of "The Lost Chord", when at the crucial crescendo both upper and lower dentures fell from his lips. Nothing daunted, Bill caught the errant prosthetics like the good slip catcher he had been in his cricketing days, and replaced them in a flash, saying sotto voce for the audience, who were doubled up with laughter, "Aaargh ye thought ye'd got me there, didn't ye" and resumed the ballad with barely a second's interruption.

Cricket and the weather

Another of Bill's special interests was cricket. He was delighted when a neighbour took him to Northampton to watch the County's best, but his real love was the village side. Bill was a noted long range weather forecaster, full of old sayings and saws about clouds, oaks and shepherd's delights. His predictions of more immediate meteorological events were always apparent from the positioning of his deckchair at home cricket matches. If it was on the boundary all would be well and the weather could be relied on. If he watched from his porch less clement weather was likely.

Mattie

Mention of Bill would be incomplete without reference to his sterling wife, Mattie, a genuine Character in her own right. Five years older than Bill she spoke with the rich singsong brogue of the remote West Coast of Ireland, 500 miles from Evenley, in a complete contrast to Bill's lovely Northamptonshire burr. As Bill tended his allotment diligently so Mattie was a wonderful preserver, bottler, jam maker and expert in all kinds of home produce. The Bugginses were keen apiculturists and their pure Northamptonshire honey featured on the shelves of favoured neighbours and friends. Moreover there is no record (other than Bill and Mattie) of anyone being stung by their bees.

Telephoning

Mattie, when excited, was difficult to understand. As the Buggins house had no telephone, when Mattie needed to speak to her family in remote Western

Ireland she would ask a neighbour to get the number for her as STD had not been invented. Mattie's family lived in Schull and on one occasion the conversation went like this.

Neighbour: I want to make a call to Schull 6 in Ireland, please.
English operator: Go ahead, please.
Irish operator: Trying to connect you.
Silence
Irish Operator: I am sorry , there is no reply from Schull 6.....but I do happen to know that Schull 6 is out and can be obtained on Schull 8.

Will I be putting you through?

Golden wedding
Bill and Mattie lived long enough to celebrate their Golden Wedding which was a grand family occasion.

Bill and Mattie's Golden Wedding

With the passage of time they became less active and it was sad to see her being pushed by the faithful Leslie in her wheelchair some years after Bill had died. When Bill died in 1976 the Church and approaches were packed, true testimony to a very remarkable Character.

The Copping family

Reg's parents came to Evenley in the early 1900's and his father worked at Evenley Hall as gardener and forester for Major Allan. They lived at no. 47 The Green. Fred, Reg's brother also lived there. Reg, who had served in the RAF, married Betty Seaton, whose parents, Jack and Hilda, lived in 48 and they moved in with them. Betty's mother was a Golding who lived at Turweston before marrying Betty's father. When Betty's father died Reg and Betty, who had meanwhile moved into 49, moved into 48, and rented out 49. Number 46 was also owned by the Coppings and rented to Mrs. Stinton. Thus for a time the Coppings owned four houses on the South side of the Green which became known as "Coppings Row"

Reg and Betty had four sons, Roger, Trevor, Steve and Martin. Steve married Joy who worked at Evenley Hall Childrens' home. Sadly none of them live in Evenley any longer. Betty loved Wimbledon and each year she would take a fortnight's holiday to watch the tennis on television and the boys had to look after themselves.

All the boys loved and were good at cricket, a talent probably inherited from their Great Grandfather Golding. There is a bench on the Green commemorating Reg & Betty Copping.

Reg Copping enjoying a pint

The Fox family

Stanley and Kitty Fox bought Evenley Fields Farm in 1955 and moved there from Hinton-in-the-Hedges. Stanley's mother was originally from Aynho and his Grandfather moved from Lower Aynho Grounds to Hinton. Stanley served on the Parish Council and was Chairman for a number of years.

They had a son, Nigel, and a daughter, Jackie. Nigel was born in 1953 at

Rookery Farm, Duck End, Hinton-in-the-Hedges, went to Sibford School and had a very successful rugby career. He started off playing for Oxford County Juniors. He was then chosen to play for the England Under 15 School Boys in Wales and at Twickenham. He then played for the England Under 18 Youth Team in its match at Pontypool.

At 17 he was in the Oxford Senior City Team. At 19 he played for Northampton. His last game for Northampton was in 1988 and altogether he made 274 first team appearances. He played in the Front Row.

After that he coached the team for 2 years and then retired to farm at Evenley Fields farm.

Parish Councillor

Nigel was on the Parish Council for 23 years and Chairman for 11 years during which time he saw and had to deal with many of the changes in the village written about in this book. While on the Council they succeeded in getting a roundabout built on the A43 at the top of Broad Lane. Evenley also won the "Best Kept Village" competition.

Musical career

Nigel started a band in 1970 with Syd Twynham, Danny Schaeffer, an American, and Robbie Holmes, drummer. Nigel plays the bass guitar and there are now three in the band, although there were originally four. They are The Montanas.

They went to America to play in California and they played in the Banbury Blues Festival. They have played in Devon, Cornwall, London and, of course, Evenley where they are extremely popular. In 2008 they organised a very successful gig in the Village Hall to raise money for the replacement of trees on the Green and raised about £700.

Syd Twynham, a brilliant guitarist, one of the original four, moved to London, where he played with Liquid Gold, which achieved worldwide chart success with a string of hits. Syd joined MUD in the early eighties but returned to Liquid Gold when they were at no. 2 in the UK singles chart with "Dance Yourself Dizzy" He is now back in Evenley and lives on the Green.

Jackie

Jackie, Nigel's sister, came to Evenley in 1955. She moved to Canada in 1971 where she was first a secretary and then worked in a sawmill for four years where she obtained her Lumber Grading Certificate. She then became a hotel receptionist and finally started and ran her own cleaning business for 12 years. She returned to Evenley in 1997 and became a Parish Councillor in 2010, does "bed and breakfast" and is a keen bicyclist having tackled the "Coast to Coast" challenge with two friends, described elsewhere in the book.

The Franklin Family

Vernon Franklin was a great great grandson of Benjamin Franklin the American Statesman and scholar, who, incidentally, also found time to invent the lightening conductor. He married Edith and they bought Franklin's Farm in 1938 in the Evenley Hall Estate sale.

Their son Richard, who married Helen, worked on the farm along with Peter, Richard's brother. Richard took over the farm from his father and worked it until it was sold in about 1989 to Lance Harman. The farm originally had pigs, sheep and cattle, but in the latter years converted to arable. When the farm was sold Richard became groundsman at Stowe. He sadly died in 1998.

The houses in the development were built in 1989 and in 1999 the development was named Franklin's Yard in his memory.

Edith used to organise whist drives and dances in the Men's Club, which is now the Shop. Peter Franklin, Richard's elder brother, looked after the cricket pitch to an enormously high standard. If there was a very hot dry spell he used to get up in the middle of the night to water it. It was known as the best cricket pitch in Northamptonshire.

Helen Franklin still lives in Franklin's Yard and her son, Nigel, lives next door.

The Martin family

Vaughan and Wilf's great grandfather David James Martin came to the village in the 1920's and rented College Farm. Josiah Elisha Martin, his son, moved to Post Office Row in 1930 and helped his father on the farm. His sons, David and Raymond, who was Vaughan and Wilf's father, took over the farm from Josiah.

The family have lived in seven houses in Evenley. Gulliver's Cottage where a Miss Gulliver, an aunt, lived, College Farm, The Barn House, Post Office Row, 1 and 8 Meadow View (now School Lane) and Boughton Terrace.

Josiah was on the Parish Council in about the early 1950's. David James was in the Salvation Army and looked after two Barnado's children.

Maureen Findlay, a cousin, went to the village school, where Mrs Jans was headmistress. Some of the school children used to go to the vicarage where

Mrs. Monks had formed the Coral League. They knitted eye bandages and painted pictures for calendars which could be sold for money for Africa. The children also used to go to Evenley Hall to be taught the steps for dancing round the Maypole, which they did on 1st May.

Vaughan and Rachel have two sons, Jamie and Lee. They have all played cricket for Evenley and even hit the ball over the roofs of some of the houses on the Green!

The Robbins family

Brian and Myrtle have lived in Evenley for 48 years. Myrtle's parents and great grandparents also lived in the village. The house Brian and Myrtle live in was on a strip of land Myrtle's great-uncle Albert owned. He owned all the land facing the Green. The allotments behind were rented or owned by people living in various cottages. Uncle Albert's house was built in 1949. Gradually the allotments were sold at inflated prices.

Myrtle remembers Eddie Mansfield, who had farmland by the Red Lion walking across the Green with two buckets hanging from a wooden yoke. A sensible way to carry heavy loads!

School

Myrtle and her brother Tom went to the village school as did her father, his aunts and uncles. In his aunts' and uncles' time the village schoolmaster was a Mr. Shelford. In Charles Sheppard's time (Myrtle's father) Miss Pengelly was there. When Myrtle went to the school Miss Care was the only teacher and there was one classroom for children from 5 – 11 years of age. Charles Sheppard was a keen cricketer and is in the 1925 team photograph.

An unusual discipline

During the war soldiers were billeted in Evenley Hall and camouflaged tanks were parked along the drive. Myrtle and Tom lived with their Aunt Laura during the week at Elm Tree Farm, the other side of the A43. They used to pass the tanks on Evenley Hall drive every morning on their way to school, carrying their gas masks.

Miss Care was a very strict teacher and if Myrtle and Tom were one minute late Myrtle was given two smacks on her hand, one for herself and one for her brother because Miss Care said he was too young to be smacked. One day Miss Care said "Tom, you are old enough now to have your own smack". They were never late again!

Ray Roycroft

Ray was born in 1931 in London. He, his sister Betty, and his parents moved to Evenley because Ray's father had a sister, Mattie (who married Bill Buggins), who had come over from Ireland to work at Rectory farm.

He is not certain how old he was when this happened but he remembers that he was still in a pram and reckons he has probably lived in Evenley longer than anyone else.

Ray went to school in what is now the Village Hall and was taught by Miss Care until he was 11 and then went to Brackley Senior School.

The children had to walk to the school then and if it was fine they took a short cut across Evenley Park.

Work

Ray spent most of his working life in farming, first labouring for Fred Chattel then Humphrey's and finally at Twyford Seeds where he was for 33 years.

Marriage to Dorothy

Ray married Dorothy in 1966. She came to the village to work as a cook at Hall Farm. Ray lived in Dormer Row then. When they got married they lived in the annexe at Hall Farm until they got the cottage at 21 The Green where he still lives. Dorothy sadly died in 1988.

Reliant Robin

Ray has been a great supporter of the Robin Reliant cars. He has nearly covered all the colours of the rainbow with orange, blue, yellow, (like Del Boy) red and green.

Ray with his car in the big freeze of 2009

Memories

Ray has many memories of Evenley from the windmill driven water pump behind Church Lane which nearly removed his fingers to the two bombs which fell on the village during the war. One fell on present day Rudgeway and the other, which killed six cows, where

Church Leys is now. Ray used to go rabbiting where the Pocket Park is – made more dangerous because there was an ammunition dump in the big tin sheds there.

He remembers playing pool, darts and cards in the Club Room which is where the Shop and Post Office is and attending dances and receptions there with a big open fire at the far end. It cost a shilling a month to be a member.

Sunday lunch

Ray has been known to visit the Red Lion and when he was first married he agreed with Dorothy that they would have their Sunday Lunch on Mondays so that a convivial Sunday could be enjoyed!

Retirement

Since retiring Ray helps many people, shopping for them, gardening and "sorting out". For 24 years he worked for the Parish Council cutting the grass around the Green, the Churchyard and the rest of the village. He took particular pride in preparing the area of the War memorial for the Armistice Day service.

Ray, both in his working life and after his retirement, has been one of the stalwarts of Evenley, a great help to many people and a source of much information about the past of the village

Cicely Spencer

Cicely Spencer has already featured in our book "Tales of Evenley" where we published her memoir of her life in Evenley, until she died age 97 in 1999. However that story told us more about her view of Evenley than it did about her.

This is an opportunity to put on record some personal facts about one of the great "Characters" (how she would hate this) of Evenley.

Not only was she seen as the Lady of the Manor but she also chaired the Parish Council in her time and was a major influence in the Church and the village.

So often before making an important decision people would say "What would Cicely think of this?" or "I don't think Cicely would approve do you?"

Cicely had the proverbial heart of gold and was interested in other people and did so much for them. Even in her nineties she would drive (a very risky event) her "old people", aged in their seventies and eighties, to Church. Her technique for crossing the A43, before the roundabout was made was simply to put her foot on the accelerator and charge, a technique adapted by at least one resident today to circumnavigate the new roundabout. She was eventually forced to give up driving "because the car had failed its M O T".

As well as her driving skills Cicely was also something of a poet and here is one of her many delightful sallies.

" Ode upon meeting my friends out exercising

We all know it is a herd of buffalo
of lions there is a pride
also a swarm of bees
but who are these who ride – astride?
behold it surely is
a cavalcade of Croperleys!

N.B. in my dictionary an ode is "a lyric poem of lofty style!!!! "

Invitations to tea

Her invitations to tea were much sought after but slightly hazardous. Cicely did not recognise summer time and kept her watch on GMT throughout the year, so it was a bit of a challenge to know exactly when to arrive, particularly when the clocks had just changed one way or the other.

Having arrived you were treated to the most magnificent feast; incredibly thinly sliced cucumber and tomato sandwiches, unbelievable marmalade cake and a good nudge when it was time to leave.

Woe betide you if you noticed that there were no fitted carpets; rugs were the only acceptable floorcovering. But you had to see the family portrait which had disappeared some years ago and had been discovered by her grandson, Stephen, in an auction in Kirkby Lonsdale and returned to the fold.

Woe betide you also if you were a cohabiting unmarried couple. However well you got on with Cicely you would not get the prized invitation to tea until you had taken that trip to the altar.

The Woodgates

Bill and Joan Woodgate moved to Evenley in 1963. They were joined in 1964 by Joan's mother, Dorothy Morley, and over the next 20 years by other members of Joan's side of the family. The Woodgates first lived in Borton's Close (now Finches Cottage). Their sons, Charles and Nicholas went to Magdalen College School. Joan kept horses and gave riding lessons. Dorothy designed the stork margarine logo in 1920. She died in 1996, in her hundredth year. Bill was on the Parish Council, was President of the Cricket Club and played hockey for Bicester. He encouraged many of the young lads in the village to join the hockey club. Bill's final ambition was to outlive his mother-in-law, which he did, but it was a close run thing.

UNUSUAL OR EXTRAORDINARY ACHIEVEMENTS BY RESIDENTS

There are also a number of people who live or have lived in the village who do or have done unusual or extraordinary things which have contributed to village life and pride in our village. These stories, some of which are in their own words, show the amazing width of interests and commitment in the village.

Carolyn Oley's Ordination and John's Pilgrimage

Carolyn and John came to the village from Herefordshire in 1988. They had lunch in the Pub, looked over the Green and decided this was where they wanted to live. Their house is in Dormer Row where the gardens are offset. The garden of number 5 is behind its house but being a little wider extends behind number 6. As the Row extends so the overlap increases until the garden of number 10 is entirely behind numbers 11 and 12. It is rather quirky.

Carolyn was asked to help with organising the Sunday School in the Village Hall shortly after her arrival in Evenley. Fiona Mason and Madeline Furnivall had been running it for a long time but Fiona was leaving the village and Madeline wanted to retire from it. Carolyn and Chris Cousins picked up the baton and ran it for many years, longer than they care to remember!

John has played the organ in the village church for many years. He has also encouraged other parishioners to take up running. John ran regularly in the Evenley Fun Run and has completed a number of marathons without suffering a single blister.

The Pilgrimage

Whilst John and Carolyn were holidaying in Galicia, John read about the famous pilgrimage, the Camino, to Santiago de Compostela and the call grew. Carolyn's brother, Mark, who resides in Alaska, decided to walk the 500 miles with John. Each carried a scallop shell, a symbol of the Pilgrim, tied to their rucksacks. They started in France at St Jean Pied de Port whence they took the 'Route Napoleon' over the high pass through the Pyrenees. Pilgrims stay at 'refugios' run by local churches or charities where for 5 euros you can get a bed in a large dormitory with a number of snoring pilgrims. Occasionally the 5 euros included a meal, not always of very high quality. Following one dreary day in the rain and a particularly cold night in the refugio, John and Mark decided comfort was needed. The next night they booked into a Parador in San Domingo and luxuriated in warm baths, good food and hot chocolate. Sadly John's knees forced them to abandon the pilgrimage at Burgos, after only 200 miles, so they travelled by train and used all the unspent 5 euros on a couple of nights in the famous Parador in Santiago. John completed the pilgrimage in 2010.

The Queen's Jubilee Tea Party

Ken Ames asked Carolyn whether she could organize the Queen's Jubilee tea party for the children of the village. She asked how many children she should cater for and the answer came back "Haven't a clue". So she asked twenty friends from the village to buy frilly plates and each make six jellies, plus one cake and a plate of sandwiches. On the day Frances Reader and Buddy Jell helped to set up the tables and lay places for fifty children. The rain stopped after lunch and many cakes, jellies and sandwiches arrived. Forty eight children sat down for tea and made a lovely sight on the Green. After tea they all got down to watch a Punch and Judy show and their parents were invited to enjoy the remains of the tea. Hardly a crumb was left!

Carolyn's Ordination

The call to the priesthood is a mysterious thing. Carolyn was already a pastoral assistant when she went to see the Director of Ordinands in Peterborough in 2004 about the possibility of being ordained, but because of her family commitments she decided the time was not right, especially as she had a suspicion that the Church of England was only really interested in appointing men. However, in spite of this delay, the persistent call continued to intrude so eventually the lengthy process of approval for ordination came on track. This resulted in going to a Selection Conference involving three days of interviews at Ely. She was told to expect the results in ten days. The call from the Bishop came eventually, late in the evening on the last possible day, just as she had given up hope. Acceptance for Ordination training resulted in three years at Ripon College, Cuddlesdon near Oxford. It was one of the happiest high spots of her life. After three years she had finished training and passed the course and the Bishop sent her to Blakesley, to assist the Rector of the Lambfold Benefice as a curate. When Gill Barker announced at the Evenley PCC meeting that Carolyn was to serve in the Lambfold benefice, a puzzled parishioner, who had genuinely misheard, asked the question "Why is Carolyn going to the Landfill benefice?

In July 2009 Carolyn was ordained as a priest.

Jessica Church's One Year Contract to work in Saudi Arabia

In 1978 I did the equivalent of joining the French Foreign Legion. I went to work for an American oil company in the deserts of Saudi Arabia.

Step into the unknown

It was a huge step into the unknown. What I knew about it was that women were second class citizens, had to wear concealing clothing, were not allowed to drive, no pork or alcohol was permitted and there was heavy press censorship. I was also fed other edifying bits of information like every Friday in the market square heads, feet and hands were chopped off – the severity of the punishments fitting the crimes. All of this was true – except that even though alcohol was illegal many people profited hugely by distilling and selling 100% proof 'moonshine'. A very risky business which could and did lead to flogging, imprisonment and/or deportation.

Arrival

On arrival the first thing that hits you is the heat. It's like a great wet, heavy, hot blanket. Then the smells. Food, spices, unwashed bodies. Then the noise. Jabbered Arabic which, until your ears get tuned, sounds as if there are no consonants at all in the language.

At the airport I and my suitcases were grabbed by an Arab in robes and head dress and bundled into a car. After about twenty minutes he stopped the car, jumped out and went round kicking the tyres while I sat in the back thinking about white slave traffic.

We drove into the desert. Away from the airport and the debris of dead bits of machinery, scrubby bushes and half finished buildings the scenery becomes transformed. The sand dunes stretch away into infinity, the wind rippling the surface and creating gentle, rolling, treeless hills. Very beautiful, very remote and very frightening. Dotted about in the distance were the flares of the oil drilling rigs.

Suddenly, in the middle of nowhere and springing up out of the arid landscape of the sands was a 'camp' complete with palm trees, bougainvillea, frangipani, lights, streets, houses and buildings. I had apparently arrived. And I stayed for ten years.

Jose Golding and her ascent of Mount Kilimanjaro

Jose Golding and five girl friends set themselves the challenge of ascending Mount Kilimanjaro both for themselves and to raise money for the Royal Marsden Hospital.

They started extensive training in the Lake District, on Snowdon, Dartmoor and Exmoor and were all ready to go in the autumn of 2007.

They left Heathrow for Nairobi in the afternoon of 25th September and after an overnight flight a further flight took them to Kigongoni where they must have been relieved to have a day's leisure before departing on a day safari.

They then transferred to Kilimanjaro Mountain Resort for a briefing, insurance check and a session with Kenya Health and Safety on the dangers ahead.

The first hike - Saturday

On Saturday they met the porters, twenty in total with three guides and a cook - four support staff for each girl! Then they had their first hike, from Rongai Trailhead on a route along the border between Kenya and Tanzania, although Kilimanjaro is actually in Tanzania. This was an ascent from 1950 meters to 2600 meters, a total of 650 meters but a lot more on the ground – and the legs. The guides were careful to tell everyone to go "pole pole" i.e. "slowly slowly", which they did, particularly towards the end of each day.

Temperatures fall - Sunday

Sunday started with an "early cup of tea in bed", much needed after that first hike, followed by a further ascent, this time of 1000m. This was the first time they needed added clothes as temperatures fell quite steeply in the late afternoon and during the night. They were also told to drink lots of water and eat carbohydrates to build up their strength.

Altitude sickness - Monday

Monday took them up to Mawenzi Tarn Camp, a short steep climb up grassy slopes. They were warned that this would be the first day when they would probably experience altitude sickness and indeed they did. Plans were always in position for the evacuation of anyone suffering seriously. Apart from breathlessness and nausea other side effects are headaches, loss of appetite and irregular digestion.

The camp was tented, consisting of a living room, kitchen and sleeping tents for two in each, all carried and put up by the "boys", and of a very high standard, as was the cooking.

Preparation for the summit - Tuesday

The next day, Tuesday, was mainly preparation for the summit on the Wednesday although there was first a 520m. ascent to a height of 4759m. The objective was to get to camp early, rest, eat lots to build up energy for the final ascent and get to bed by 6.00pm.

The summit - Wednesday

Throughout the whole ascent they had good weather, cold at night, increasingly frosty, until near the summit when it was frosty throughout the day as well.

On Wednesday they had to ascend 1146 m., some of it through a rocky terrain. They started at 11.00 on the Tuesday evening and had about five or six hours trudging up well graded zigzags with regular stops to reach the first summit of Gilmans at a height of 5681m. Jose fell a bit behind at one stage but, as she says, sheer obstinacy drove her on and she made the summit without too much difficulty.

The sunrise and the views were magnificent and she could see for many miles on a glorious morning. She felt a tremendous sense of achievement both for herself and for her fundraising, helped by sponsorship, for the Royal Marsden. She had ascended 5681 m. in four days.

She tried to phone her slightly worried husband, Kim, but there was no signal from the top. However, she was able to reassure him and give news of her success on the way down.

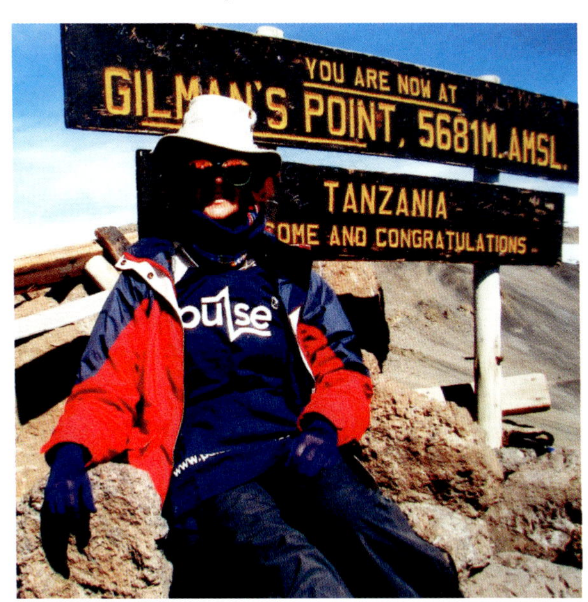

Jose (yes it really is her) on the top of Kilimanjaro

The descent

The next day saw a much quicker descent to base camp and a welcome from the "boys" who did a victory dance on meeting Jose, then a rest and a welcome shower.

A few more days of relaxation in Kenya and then the plane home and back to Evenley.

The group's final triumph was in having raised £18,000 for various charities; Jose's being the Royal Marsden.

Would she do it again? A cautious "Yes" but with more emphasis on the breathing training in preparation for the high altitudes; after all it was the equivalent of two thirds of the way up Everest!

Carrie, Jackie and Clare's Coast to Coast bicycle ride

A short bit from Wheeliegirls about our Coast to Coast. We'd like to say a huge thank you to everyone who encouraged us before we went, sent emails to wish us well and for your sponsorship, so far we have raised about £2000 for BYHP (Banbury Young Homeless People) which is amazing. THANK YOU.

Setting off

After travelling up on the Tuesday we set off on Wednesday 20th May from St Bees on a cloudy day, travelling through country lanes towards Keswick. At our cafe stop that day another punter was so impressed she gave us £10; we must look honest! Our first walk of the trip was up part of Winlatter Pass, but we did manage to cycle most of it. Kevin and the camper were suitably positioned, as he was each day, for a lunch stop before we whizzed downhill and on towards our night's stop at Troutbeck, a lovely site with brilliant power showers.

Day two

Day two saw us set off towards Penrith, again through beautiful country lanes and the University of Cumbria campus, with dry cloudy skies. We knew we had some big climbs and after lunch we launched up to Hartside, a long steady climb of 4 miles into the Pennines and I'm pleased to report that we all cycled ALL of it, much to everyone's surprise! The scenery changed from that point, becoming much more barren but the long downhill into Alston was done within 10 minutes. The three of us then found another cafe for coffee and cake whilst Kevin went on to set up camp about three miles ahead. I think that was the most 'interesting' site I've been on, nearly all static vans and we and one other caravan were squeezed in between them.

Friday

Friday started with drizzle for the first long climb (18%) of the day out of Nenthead. This used to be a big lead mining area and you could imagine the area being a hive of activity in times past with the scars of mining and derelict buildings everywhere. It all looked very bleak and desolate and walking was needed to get to the top. With very wet roads we came down the other side into Stanhope much slower so we all stayed on our bikes! The second climb up onto Stanhope moor was as steep and had sharp corners too and but the ride over the moor was brilliant and we knew once over it, that we were on the mainly downhill ride to the North Sea. Our final night's stop was just south of Castleside.

Day four

Day four was almost entirely along the Waskerley Way, a traffic free cycle path, mainly on old railway lines. After cycling nearly 40 miles each day the 25 we had to do on Saturday went very quickly and we rode into Sunderland along the river, past The Stadium of Light and into the Marina at 1.30pm to be met with champagne and greeted by excited pets and partners who I don't think had been fully convinced we'd all finish the whole thing!

Again?

Could we do it again? YES, and we are already researching where to cycle next year. It is a great way to see the countryside, everyone was very friendly and encouraging on route, so watch this space for our next venture.

An anonymous midnight rider

Someone in the village is addicted to riding out at midnight. Preferring moon-lit nights that person has ridden as far as Steeple Claydon and Northbrook, (about 14 miles each), then staying the rest of the night with a friend and returning home in the morning.

They once paused for a rest by an old railway bridge and suddenly found what appeared to be a white plastic supermarket bag floating up towards them. It turned out to be a white barn owl which was as surprised as the rider. It settled about two feet away and they eyeballed each other. It, the owl, raised its eyebrows, or perhaps they both did, and in a short while it turned away and floated off in a most relaxed way, reminiscent of David Attenborough's encounter with the King Penguin.

Rob and Eddie's Lands End to John O'Groats bicycle trip

On 6th July 2008 Rob and Eddie left Lands End in wind and rain. They were bicycling all the way to John o'Groats and raising money for charity.

The trip

The first day they rode 130 miles and reached Exeter. They had a camper van following them as support and they slept and ate in it most of the time. The route took them on to Staunton, near Whitchurch, Bolton le Sand, Moffat, Loch Lomond, Ben Nevis, Inverness, Dingwall and finally John o'Groats.

The weather was atrocious most of the way. They only wore shorts on two days out of the 10 they took to get there. In Glencoe they had to call the motor home to come so that they could put on more clothes as it was so cold. From Gretna to Moffat they had 8 miles of virtual cloudburst. The spray was streaming off their wheels and there was a river flowing down the road towards them. On the A74 Carlyle to Gretna they found themselves on a dual carriageway with the traffic going very fast. It was so unpleasant they quickly left the A74 to find a quieter road.

Rob and Eddie at John O'Groats

Flat tyres

They only had two flat tyres, amazingly within a very short time of each other – both on Shap Fell and each one, of course, having to be changed in the rain. Someone on a skateboard passed them going the other way skateboarding all the way from John o'Groats to Lands End!

The finish

Jackie Fox and Sue McGourley were going to surprise them at John o'Groats, but had to contact them to ask when they were going to arrive. Rob and Eddie could have done it in 9 days, but they delayed arriving for a day so that Jackie and Sue could be there with champagne, flags, etc. Jackie had cooked some meals for them for the beginning of their journey and then delivered some to the motor home when they were half way.

It was a great achievement in awful weather. Rob lost nearly a stone in weight, but raised £2000 for cystic fibrosis and Eddie also raised £2000 for his Masonic Lodge.

Rob rode as an amateur for nine years and a pro for six. He rode three times for England, for Raleigh's first road team and also did the Tour of Britain Milk Race in the 1960's. He also rode in the Tour of Yugoslavia and a race in Holland and in his career won many trophies.

Michael Ewens' strange experiences as an Oxford Bursar

After several decades in the British Army becoming an Oxford Bursar certainly lived up to the promise of a challenging, stimulating and rewarding second career.

There is little doubt that working in a College founded in 1509 surrounded by bright and sometimes demanding Fellows and students College life did often pose testing moments, of which some might be seen as amusing. However, incidents such as these, I came to understand, were very much in the tradition of Oxford.

Strange excuses

An example concerns rooms. Although in subsequent years the selection of rooms is by ballot, in their first year students are allocated rooms in college by the accommodation staff. As a general rule this systems works particularly well although sometimes it can cause 'unhappiness' to certain students. When this happens resolution often necessitates adjudication on the validity of the excuse for a room change by the Domestic Bursar.

In my time these ranged from the birds singing in the foliage immediately outside the window were too disturbing, to the mobile telephone reception in the room not being adequate. But, arguably the most original excuse was that, after measurement, the occupant had discovered the magnetic lines of force in the room were out of equilibrium with his psyche. Perhaps it was my facial expression that gave away my private thoughts because his next statement was that I appeared 'not to be taking his complaint seriously.'

Changing rooms is not as easy as one might think as it requires a deal of re-organisation, re-publishing of location lists and significant disturbance to other students, but to those who might be wondering, all the above examples did have the desired effect and rooms were changed.

A large caterpillar!

Nevertheless, over the years I learnt that even Domestic Bursars can experience terms when all goes well and whilst they still remain the butt of student humour it can be benevolent almost, dare I say, bordering on the mildly appreciative. This was particularly so during the last week of a Michaelmas Term.

After a particularly good party a group of students decided that it would be a good idea to chalk up at various locations on the College interior walls "friendly remarks and Christmas wishes to the Domestic Bursar". Even in their excited state they reasoned correctly that even though it was now well into the early hours of the night and quite dark it would be an advantage if they took precautions to remain unidentified.

Being bright Oxford undergraduates and aware that the College had recently upgraded the CCTV security cameras they devised a simple plan. They would form up in line, cover themselves with sheets and similar items and like a many legged caterpillar proceed fully covered from Quad to Quad stopping here and there to leave their chalked messages. The deed was done!

Arriving at College the following morning I was greeted by the Head of Security, (in Oxford Speak, the Head Porter), who told me of the night's activities and throughout the College there were indeed many chalked messages wishing the Domestic Bursar the compliments of the season. The upgraded CCTV system permitted the nights prank to be played back. It was clear to see the caterpillar with its twelve legs move from location to location whence it would stop and a hand would appear from the 'front end' and the messages would be chalked up only for the caterpillar to move on again. It was possible to trace the caterpillar's route through the College until it finally disappeared out of sight and assumed safety from discovery.

However, all that was required now was a little patience, and sure enough in a few minutes 'the game was up' when by virtue of their distinctively patterned socks, strange footwear or the hastily rolled up sheet or throw they were carrying over their arm, six easily identifiable students appeared on the monitor screen. It was the Junior Common Room Committee members.

They were summoned to the Domestic Bursar's Office. I firstly thanked them for their kind seasonal wishes but insisted that they cleaned the walls before the Dean was made aware of what happened. I was asked how I knew it was them. I explained. I was then asked if I was going to report them to the Dean, I replied that I thought a more appropriate 'punishment' would be for them to listen to a short explanation of the principles of camouflage which I recalled from my basic army training.

I like to think that many of these 'caterpillar legs' are now captains of industry and in positions of very great national and probably international importance.

The Wild West (Evenley style) by Jessica Church

What a lovely country sound – the slow clip clop of horses' hooves passing along the lane under my bedroom window. Except that it was three o'clock in the morning and horses don't usually clip clop around at that hour. The temptation was strong to dive back down under the duvet but the conscience prickled with the fear that this lone horse, plodding up and down the lane looking for a destination, might end up on the A43.

Gathering the posse

Probably the most sensible thing to do would have been to phone the police but that brilliant solution never entered my head. The nearest horse owner I knew was Jackie Fox so I phoned her. Personally I would never answer the phone at three o'clock in the morning since the one time I did the voice of what was almost certainly a serial killer on cocaine said 'have you got my stuff?' But thankfully she answered. I was hoping she would say 'go back to bed I'll look after it' but, quite understandably, what she actually said was 'I'll meet you in the lane'. So there we were in our pyjamas; I couldn't produce so much as a piece of string and Jackie turned up with a dog lead.

The round up

The horse was having nothing to do with us and promptly took off into Church Leys. Jackie went off to find the owners and I stayed behind with instructions to 'head it off'. 'Head it off?' - by this time the horse was so spooked I was more likely to get trampled . I was then joined by Lee Balderstone, also in her nightwear, who had been woken up by the commotion. Between us we did indeed head it off but unfortunately into Rectory Farm garden. We were then joined by an alarmed and startled Jane Gibb (similarly attired) who had looked out of her bedroom window and seen the terrified animal churning up her lawn.

Resort to the Cavalry

Mercifully the Cavalry, consisting of Jackie, the owners and their companion pony, appeared at high speed at which time the local 'cowgirls' were able to break up the pyjama party and go home.

Our apologies to anyone who might have been enjoying the entertainment from their upstairs windows – the Evenley Round Up will NOT be an annual event.

Andrew Bullock's Brazilian Trek for UNICEF

Our former ERA Chairman undertook a trek, with thirty four others, across Brazil on behalf of UNICEF. It was across the Bocaina National Park from San Jose de Barreiro to Mambucaba – Angrados Reis. This is a central route made in stones by slaves at the end of the 18th century, originally used by the Guaianazes Indians and later by troops leading donkeys packed with gold from the Minas Gerais and coffee from the vale paraibano. This is why it is called "Trilha Do Ouro" or "The Gold Route".

The trek took five days and covered 125kms. They were led by a guide, Sebolla, who gave each of them three pine tree seeds to plant on the way.

Their accommodation was cramped, simple and sometimes without electricity, making it difficult to dry wet clothes. They ate simple food – chicken and rice and for lunch dried bread with sweetcorn paste.

They walked through rainforests with beautiful flowers, butterflies, insects and birds. They encountered poisonous spiders, aggressive bees, a giant snail the size of a tennis ball, ticks and a very venomous snake which slithered right in front of Andrew and stopped to look at him! The guide gently persuaded it to move on.

They suffered from large blisters, cuts, bruises, strains, heat stroke, exhaustion, being soaked through by torrential rain many times, a major thunder storm and crossing a river in a steel cage. They swam in amazing waterfalls with water crashing down 150m or so in warm sunshine, but had to climb up steep mountains of 1600m above sea level and then down again on the trail. However, it was all worth it for the spectacular scenery.

They all survived and reached the end of the trek. They raised over £40,000 for UNICEF's Inspiring Young Minds programme which supports sports projects and encourages children to attend school and avoid drugs.

A Silly Sailor

One person who wished to remain anonymous asked if he could provide details of the stupidest thing he had ever done and this is it!

He set off with a friend one glorious morning in the hot summer of 1959 to sail from Waldringfield, (mentioned in the Domesday book which should have been a warning), on the river Deben in Suffolk to Great Yarmouth in a sixteen foot half decked dinghy to spend a fortnight sailing on the Suffolk and Norfolk Broads. The distance was about 75 miles by sea.

Crossing the bar

Leaving Waldringfield at 04.30 in the morning they careered down the Deben towards the mouth of the river with a strong ebb tide, hitting one underwater obstacle but without serious damage. At the mouth there is a sand bar across the exit with a very limited gap for safe passage. (This may have been the very bar that Tennyson referred to in his poem "Crossing the bar" and should have been a further warning!) The idea was that you steered the boat for the gap and went through smoothly. Unfortunately at that time on this beautiful morning there was virtually no wind to give steerage way and the tide was extremely strong at the mouth of the river.

So over the bar instead of through the gap went the dinghy and by incredible good luck it did not capsize, which was just as well as there was absolutely no one about at that hour nor had the mobile phone been invented.

Getting pooped

Nothing ventured they pressed on until they were opposite Aldeburgh at which point they realised that they did not have a map of the coastline and would have no means of knowing when they had reached Great Yarmouth. Apart from knowing where they had got to, they had to arrive at Great Yarmouth at the right time so that the new tide would take them into the Broads because they had no engine.

So they decided to go ashore at Aldeburgh and buy a map. Easier said than done. Arriving at the beach bow on, although the sea was mild the boat was pooped; i.e. a wave came over the stern partially filling the boat with water and ruining most of the provisions.

Moreover no map of the coast could be found in the town and the only item available was a printed tea towel or washing up cloth, which fortunately had both Aldeburgh and Great Yarmouth printed on it.

Portuguese man of War

At sea again and rather wet the next object sighted was a Portuguese Man of War moving in the same direction. This jellyfish or near jellyfish is extremely dangerous to swimmers near the shore let alone to two lunatics out at sea. So great care was taken not to capsize.

Land Ho!

The next worry was that the boat had no navigation lights and the torch, which could have been shone on the sail in an emergency, was full of water. However good time was made and the flood tide took the dinghy into Oulton Broad where they moored.

Dinner and disaster

Dinner was to be a twelve egg omelette between the two of them and, believe it or not, on cracking the eggs directly into the pan the twelfth was bad! And furthermore his friend rammed a jetty when stopping one evening and the wooden planked boat sprung a minor leak. Result; they had to wake up at 2.00 a.m. every night to bale out otherwise they would have been floating down the river and out to sea on their lilos!

Common sense returns

The return trip was made by car, leaving more sensible sailors to bring the boat back to Waldringfield.

Three stories of flying – varying from luxury to sheer terror!

Jessica Church's flight on Concorde

There are times in life when you have to do something mad, expensive, purposeless and reckless – just because you want to. I flew on Concorde, just before she was decommissioned because I had been in love with that beautiful piece of engineering ever since her maiden flight in 1976.

Before leaving Heathrow for New York (economy), I stayed the night in West London under the Concorde flight path. That evening the Test Match was being played at Lords. The television match commentator said "and dead on time here comes Concorde" and with one eye on the television and another on the skies outside the flat, there she was above me and unbelievably I was going to be on board in four days time.

On September 9 2003 I checked in at the special Concorde desk at Kennedy airport for the flight home and went through for breakfast. Champagne, Buck's Fizz, smoked salmon, eggs, bacon, 'grits', croissants and anything else you could possibly want but shouldn't have.

The cabin was narrow and quite cramped and the windows tiny. The food and drink kept coming. And this of course was quite shortly after the VIP Concorde departure lounge breakfast! A five course gourmet meal and a choice of seven champagnes, seven white burgundies, seven clarets, four red burgundies and one port. Makes you wonder how they had room for the engines. The air hostesses were a professional lot but had obviously been rewarded for their length of service with BA by being allocated the Concorde flight. However it was the flight I was there for and it was utterly amazing and thrilling.

After take off the plane practically stood on her tail and tore up into the sky heading towards maximum height and twice the speed of sound – Mach 2. The speed was recorded on a screen so everyone knew when it had been reached and the captain came on the intercom to give some technical details and a few emotional words about the sheer brilliance of the unique aircraft. Inside the plane there was absolutely no sensation of speed. The curve of the horizon glowed through the window. This and more must be what astronauts see.

Because the flight was so short – about 2 ½ hours – you feel quite cheated when it is all over and you land at Heathrow. The last flight was in October 2003. The end of passenger supersonic air travel and the death of something very, very, special. It was worth every penny.

Terry Stopford's emergency landing in France

Emergency over the Pyrenees

When I was an air hostess I had only been flying a short time and was on board a Viscount en route to Palma, Majorca with a crew of Captain, First Officer, Radio Officer and one other steward. It was not a large plane by today's standards and probably had about 100 people on board. Approaching the Pyrenees we ran into a ferocious electrical storm which had the plane lurching through the skies, rocking to and fro, dipping sideways and dropping like a stone in the air pockets. The lightning was flashing and huge ice balls were hammering on the plane. We were all strapped in but the steward and I were sitting facing the passengers and had to keep an expression of calm and nonchalance on our faces so as not to spread further alarm. We needed to land urgently but because of the storm all the airports within reach were closed. We were circling and rapidly running out of fuel. Unfortunately I could hear the Radio Officer practically begging Toulouse Air Traffic Control to open up a runway so that we could put down, which did not give me any comfort at all.

Safe landing

Eventually Toulouse opened up for us and we landed safely, if with force. We were surrounded by every available emergency vehicle and the escape chutes shot out from the aircraft. The steward was knocked unconscious but recovered enough to lead the passengers off down the chutes assisted by the two Officers. The Captain and I stayed until last to make sure everyone got out. I heard that one little boy having safely ejected was so excited that he asked if he could have another go!

After a shaky night in a hotel we inspected the aircraft the next day. Not only had one of the engines caught fire but the fuselage was covered in dents from the impact of the ice balls. That aircraft never flew again.

David Bush's wipe out at 35,000feet

David had a love of aeroplanes and flying from a very early age thanks to his elder brother who made and flew model aeroplanes.

Called to do his National Service at 18 years of age David volunteered for flying duties in the Royal Air Force. Following medicals and aptitude tests he was graded for training as a navigator. Fortunately he was granted 12 hours grading flying in Tiger Moths at Officer Training School and going solo after only 5½ hours he was soon re-graded to pilot training. Having gained his commission he then went on first to Basic Flying School and then to Advance Training School and gained his pilots wings after 97 hours dual instruction and 90 hours solo flying. He was 19 years and 4 months when he gained his wings.

He flew the Meteor mark 3 which was not fitted with an ejector seat and if you lost power you had no way to re-ignite your engines.

David tells his own story of a "Very Near Miss "which occurred on the 30th June 1952.

"It was mid morning on the 30th June 1952. I took off from RAF Oakington in a Meteor 3 for only the ninth time solo. I climbed all the way up to 35,000ft and then all hell broke loose as I experienced tremendous vibration from both engines and they were on fire. I immediately turned off the fuel to each engine and triggered the fire extinguishers, which fortunately put out the fires.

I then put out a Mayday Distress call and after transmitting a short message informing the controllers of my predicament. I was given my position, as over Battersea Power station and told to fly on a heading of 010 that would take me back to Oakington.

Obviously, I was losing height rapidly and although there was no cloud at 35,000ft, I could see the solid cloud cover below me. Then my luck changed and I saw a gap in the clouds with a runway directly below this gap. I immediately put the nose down and dived through the cloud. As I was descending, I recognized the airfield marking BS, which was RAF Bassingbourne. My Brother was a Senior Pilot Instructor on Canberra Bombers and operated from Bassingbourne, I thought if the runway is long enough for a Canberra it should be easy to put a Meteor down. I radioed my intention to force land at Bassingbourne and was instructed to do a wheels up landing parallel to the main runway.

You can imagine the speed that I had built up in my descent without air brakes. I had sufficient speed to fly almost a perfect circuit and brought the aircraft down as instructed alongside the main runway without blocking its use to Canberras returning from training flights, including my brother. It was estimated that the speed of impact was 350 to 400 MPH and the fire crews and the ambulance that were on the runway to meet me, needed to chase me most of the length of the airfield.

Appearing to have no ill effects from my ordeal I remember standing at the bar in the mess drinking a soft drink when my brother came in and putting two and two together having seen the wrecked Meteor when he landed, he said " please don't tell Mother or she would die".

Not long after this " Near Miss" David, having been given a wrong radio bearing to return to base, just managed to land at the American Airforce Base at Mildenhall as he was short of fuel and his engines failed as he dropped onto the runway.

A Meteor 3

Two pensioners and their ice yachting

Two Evenley pensioners have gone ice yachting in Sweden each winter for the last seventeen years. This involves each sailing a boat on ice which may be as little as six inches thick or, in a good year, a couple of feet. Speeds reached are a good forty miles an hour in temperatures sometimes as low as minus ten degrees Celsius.

The beginning

He – first sailed on the ice in the winter of 1953/54 on Steinhuder Mere in Germany in a fairly primitive boat almost put together from orange boxes and skates as there was little material of quality so soon after the war. Note the steering wheel which allowed the sailor to be comfortable and upright.

She – or rather - they took up the pastime in 1994 for no known reason. Entirely by luck they ended up with a boat, at a hotel in Sweden on a frozen lake and the help of a former Swedish ice yachting champion!

A primitive ice boat

A DN iceboat being sailed by a pensioner

The DN (and they quickly had one each) was designed before the war in 1932 as a result of a competition held by the Detroit News, hence its name a "DN" It is an altogether faster model and is sailed lying on your back which puts quite a strain on the neck. Proper training for this involves lying on the floor on your back and watching television!

Sailing

A perfect day's sailing comes with black ice, a gentle wind and sun. Because boats sail faster than the wind it is necessary to run – an increasing challenge for one pensioner - to get the boat started and then comes the "lift" as the boat exceeds the wind speed and "takes off"

As boats sail faster than the wind it is relatively easy to achieve high speeds which seem even faster as you are lying on your back in the boat and are only a foot above the ice, on a bad day with rain, sleet and ice chippings flying in your face.

Boats sail like catamarans and therefore cannot sail directly downwind but have to "reverse tack" i.e. gybe which is quite difficult, particularly where the wind changes direction as you round islands and don't know quite where you want to go or came from anyway!

Dangers

Dangers, apart from collision, are from thin ice, streams which weaken the ice, hitting a crack in the ice at an angle and sudden gusts of wind all of which can cause immersion or a capsize.

Immersion and Capsize

She has gone into the water, through the ice by hitting a crack and capsized and thrown out of the boat! He has managed to avoid any of these dangers so far.

She was sailing with a friend, but without her husband as he was ill. It was a gentle wind, but the ice was black so once going one went fast. They sailed about 2 kms, met a friend and stopped for a chat. They set off again, but she couldn't get the right angle to the wind to get going. When she finally did she saw in front of her what looked like water on the ice but since it had been -20 C the day before she was certain that it was black ice, not open water. She was wrong. She didn't want to change course to avoid it as she had just got up speed so she sailed on, only to discover that it was, indeed, a big pool of water. The boat stopped. She thought 'I must get out of the boat as the water is coming over the top' so she climbed onto the bow and gingerly put a foot over the side, prepared to swim. Her relief was enormous when her foot hit ice at the bottom of the hole and although up to the top of her thigh she managed to walk out of the hole. The boat continued to sink and because it was her friend's boat she didn't want to lose it so she hung on and tried to pull it out, but wasn't strong enough. Luckily her friend realised she hadn't sailed back with him and returned to find her. They managed to pull the boat out and she had to sail back very cold and wet, but alive.

Another time she saw a crack but failed to avoid it and went into it. Half the boat was in the water, the other half on the ice and the front runner under the ice. Again she had to climb onto the bow to get out, but this time straight onto the ice. Luckily her husband came to help her pull the boat out. This time she didn't get wet.

The capsize was in very strong wind. She had just decided to head for home as the wind was too strong to sail. She started off and an enormous gust hit her and turned the boat over throwing her onto the ice. Luckily she didn't break anything herself, just the boat, but was only bruised.

The moral of these tales is 'Don't sail too close to islands as she had in the first two cases and don't sail in very strong winds.

But it was fun!

SNIPPETS

A former Chairman of the Residents Association, who moved first to Spain and then to Italy, has been taking balloon flights. Where will he end up?

Sheila Bailey, who drew the illustrations for this book, used to compete in one day events. The trouble was her horse became so excited at the start that when they were meant to start he was too busy rearing, so she used to position him with his back to the start. This way she managed to turn him round and they were off!

Sheila, on her 29th birthday, was given a sledge hammer, pick axe and crowbar by her then husband! They had bought a 1668 derelict farmhouse in Norfolk to do up. She went round it 'tapping' the walls of the 23 rooms and when she had finished there were only 18 rooms left.

Kay Baul

One of my dreams was to swim with dolphins and I have had the good fortune to swim with them not once but twice. The first time on honeymoon in the Mexican Caribbean, was out of this world. It was a wonderful experience to be able to swim, touch, play and have a foot push from dolphins. (foot push is where you tread water whilst two dolphins swim up behind you and then place their noses under each foot and push you up and out and through the water at a great rate)

My little boy often asks me how they felt; very unique, and the only thing I can think of that is very similar is when you have peeled a hard boiled egg and the outer surface of the egg feels just like a dolphin skin.

I feel very privileged to have had such a fantastic opportunity to swim with such intelligent and friendly dolphins which I will never forget.

David and Olive Bush

David with his wife Olive moved to Evenley in 1995 and served for a while as Clerk to the Parish Council and was a founder member of the Evenley Residents Association and its first treasurer. He has always supported fund raising for the church and on one occasion held an Auction of Promises raising £2,550 entirely on his own. When asked by Pat Reeves if he could make some bird boxes for the church fete he filled a stall with many wooden items that he had made from children's picnic tables to rocking horses and raised £450 for the fete. David has for many years in his retirement collected toys and many of the village children would call to see his wonderful displays. Grandparents in the village always called when they had their grandchildren to stay with them and many went home with a souvenir of their visit.

Margo Buttery moved to Evenley with her husband, Basil, in 1967. She was already an accomplished dressmaker, but did a City and Guilds course in fashion and design at Banbury Technical College in about 1977. She then started doing weddings for friends and neighbours. She would make the dress, arrange the flowers and make and decorate the cake. In about 1994 Basil heard on the radio that there was going to be an exhibition near Oxford to do with weddings and she went. Someone there was making sugar flowers and Margo discovered that there was a course in Thame to learn how to do this. It was one of the first places in England to teach sugarcraft. She learnt with Tombi Peck, a brilliant South African and other well known people. As a result of the course Margo has made and decorated many cakes for weddings, anniversaries, christenings, birthdays etc. She makes the most beautiful sugar flowers and decorations as can be seen below.

Two of Margo's cakes

Iain Duncan Smith, when leader of the opposition, was spotted having a picnic lunch with his wife sitting on a bench on the Green, near the Shop. He is now Secretary of State for Work and Pensions.

Stuart Freestone, a keen motor cyclist, who owned first a Harley and now has a BMW Adventure (a large endure type motor cycle) has made quite a number of trips. In 2006 he went to Le Mans for the 24 hour race and later in the year to the Isle of Man just for a tour, not to compete. 2007 saw Stuart travel to Venice via eleven countries (did he get lost as two countries should have done it?) 2008 saw Scotland and Ireland covered including Stranraer, the Giant's Causeway, Londonderry, Galway and back by way of Dublin, Anglesey, Snowdonia, the Cotswolds and home to a bemused family!

Major Furlong (really), who lived at Rectory Farm, owned Reynoldstown which won the Derby in 1935 and 1936. The odds were 22/1 and 10/1 respectively. Reynoldstown lived until 1951.

Hebe Gibbs had singing roles in the West End and made commercials, including the well known "let the train take the strain". She organised the choir and taught music in Evenley

John Glendinning always wanted to be a pilot and joined the RAF after leaving school although he was unable to qualify during his three year's service. On leaving the RAF he joined Plessey and spent his spare time motor bike racing, scuba diving, taking flying lessons on a Tiger Moth and microliting. He was also training in Judo, became a 2nd dan black belt in 1958, was the county coach for Buckinghamshire and was in the squad for the Olympics. In 1980 he left Plessey and made a living in Country and Western singing under the stage name of John Glenn. This brought him into contact with Ann Oetterli and they sang together as the Peacemakers. In 1994 he got his pilot's licence and now owns a part share in a motor glider and a Zenith CH 250. He spends the rest of his leisure time Scuba diving, where he is a qualified instructor, on archery and on the occasional balloon flight. His remaining ambition is to sky-dive!

Golfers abound in Evenley. There are at least six who play regularly. Mark Proffit and Spencer Burnham, both members of Sunningdale, one of the most prestigious courses in England, each have a very low handicap. Mark has had two holes in one and Spencer one. Bob Cropley, Brian Hall and several others play at Buckingham and Bob has had a hole in one on the 8th hole. Richard Stopford and others play at Stowe and he has had a hole in one at the 9th.

Jessica Church used to play in Saudi Arabia on oiled sand, where you had to take your tee mat with you. She has also played on a mountain course in the Philippines which bordered on the then President Marcos's holiday home. If you lost a ball in the undergrowth you were quite likely to come face to face with a security guard wielding a machine gun. Not very inducive to a good score! Before that, as a schoolgirl, she had a hole in one in Devon. As with other people she thought at first that she had a lost ball.

Mo Greatbatch came to the village in 1962 having just got married to David Greatbatch, who was a builder. Her great great grandmother was Queenie who was a "character" in "Lark Rise to Candleford". Both Mo and David became involved with the cricket team and Mo used to do the teas when David played. Mo was treasurer of the club in the late 1970s and is a strong supporter. She was a Parish Councillor for three years and also worked in the pub at one time. She is one of the longer standing residents of the village and has contributed a lot to the village.

Joan and Kenneth Grundy, Jose Golding's parents, lived in the village for about 25 years. They were both on the PCC and Kenneth was Treasurer. They were early members of the Bridge Club, but were really known for initiating Beetle Drives which were very popular.. They held about 4 to 5 a year and they raised £25-30 a time for the Church. These raised over £1000 over the years.

Lance Harman owned Hill Grounds, now owned by the Cropleys, restored the barns in Church Lane and was Chairman of the Parish Council at one time. He used to organise a cricket match each year in which his team played the village. The party afterwards was reputed to be the most alcoholic ever known in the Village Hall as those present might testify!

Gina Harvey, who has lived in Evenley for 33 years, is an enthusiastic amateur archaeologist who has found Roman pottery in and around Evenley and who has worked on the mediaeval Castle Lane excavation now under Tesco. She has also worked on Deddington Castle and at the Roman villa site on the Buckingham road, among others.

She was a member of the History Group, along with Isobel Armstrong, Philip Scaysbrook and Jacqueline Simpson which wrote "Aspects of Evenley" and she wrote the chapter on Roman Evenley.

She was also involved in the 1961 NATO exercise which involved flying as a passenger in an Auster aeroplane over Germany dropping classified information to our troops in the field and delivering a coded message to a Belgian General, in Belgium, from HQ BAOR in Germany.

Another claim to fame is that she has been in the pilot's seat of an F1-11 at Upper Heyford - for a photograph!

Steve Hogarth and Linette, who is Danish, have bought Bill Buggins's house on the Green from his son Les and have completed a major restoration job to return it to its original state.

Steve is vocalist with the British Rock band, Marillion. He was formerly a keyboard player and co-lead vocalist with The Europeans and vocalist with How We Live. He links, from time to time, with Nigel Fox's Montanas for the benefit of Evenley.

Buddy Jell has lived in the village since 1974 and has lived in four different houses. She is on the Parish Council and has been instrumental in seeing that the lights round the Green are replaced by attractive ones in keeping with the age of the houses. She is also a sidesman in the Church, secretary of the Bridge Club, cuts and maintains the churchyard with Ray and supports the Pub Musical evenings. Her late husband, Ron, helped start the Fun Run, raised money with Vaughan Jones for Brackley Cottage Hospital and supported the cricket.

Jonathan Kelly, son of Jill and Breff, lived in Church Lane from 1979 until his marriage to Lucy Marsh (of faraway Brackley). He is a musician and plays Principal Oboe in the Berlin Philharmonic Orchestra. He has twice played in the Village Hall, first time in 1982 as a promising thirteen year old and then in 2003 following his appointment in Berlin. Jonathan was at school at nearby MCS (Lucy's father, Keith, was then headmaster) and afterwards read History at Cambridge. He played in the National Youth Orchestra of Great Britain while at school and at Cambridge played in the CUMS Orchestra and, eventually, in the European Community Youth Orchestra. Studies at the Royal Academy of Music, where he won the President's Prize, and then Paris followed. In 1991 he was appointed Principal Oboe in the City of Birmingham Symphony Orchestra under Simon Rattle where he remained until 2003 when he went to Berlin, also under Simon Rattle. He now lives there with Lucy, three daughters and a labradoodle.

Alvar Lidell

One snowy Sunday a villager and his son received a large consignment of horse manure, which was dumped on the pavement outside his house. Several people brought wheelbarrows, including Dick Bright, and the whole soggy and smelly mess was laboriously carted away.

On the return of his barrow Dick insisted that the borrowers came in to join Dick, Mollie and their house guest for a warming tincture despite wearing gum boots covered in a pungent mixture of snow, mud and manure. The house guest was Alvar Liddell, a famous newscaster, who announced many of the key events in the war against Hitler, at a time when radio was the main communication medium.

Jean Morgan, Chief Executive of South Northants Council, lives with her husband Barrie, on the Green. She recently received a hand held Enigma machine from her uncle who had been given it by a friend who had bought it at a car boot sale for a pittance.

She has donated it on behalf of her uncle to the Bletchley Park Museum where German codes were broken during the war.

Jean Morgan with the Enigma machine

Ann Oetterli, Bill Lacey's daughter, trained as a mechanic and worked for her father and also for Mike Hailwood. She also rode bikes and has won races; once in atrociously wet conditions when the rider who was meant to compete refused to do so!

Her mother, Mae Ruffell, was also a bike enthusiast and wanted to compete in a race. Her parents said she was too young so she threw her leathers out of the window to Bill, snuck out of the house and was taken to the track where she won the 1st Ladies handicap for the Wakefield Trophy off scratch. She was something of a rebel!

Ann came to the village in 1972 and has devoted her life here to saving wildlife, mainly birds, but also rescue Great Danes. She is involved with the charity R.A.I.N. which calls her when they get an injured bird and Ann collects it and takes it home. She has two aviaries with white doves, a pigeon in the conservatory, which she has had since a juvenile, two rescued poultry, one greyhound, one Great Dane and a hive of bees at the time of writing!

Frances Reader, who is married to Charles, is the most highly qualified person in the country in helping people with pulmonary and cardiac problems. She also specialises in special needs and rehabilitation. This means that she teaches older people how to prevent themselves from falling and breaking a limb. Not content with that she also teaches Pilates!

John Richardson had been in the RAMC and had served in Northern Ireland as a doctor. The Regiment gave him a leaving present but he thought it might be a bomb so he had it blown up on the Green by a bomb disposal squad from the RAF. It was a silver tankard.

Bruce Roberts who played Nick Parrish, the policeman in Home and Away, signed autographs and gave a kiss for a pound at a fete on the Green. The A43 was blocked by cars trying to get to Evenley and many were parked in nearby fields!

Betty Scaysbrook was a WAAF in the war and a great piano player. As well as playing in the Services, the village and in Brackley Antiques Centre she also played with Stephane Grappelli and for the Goon Show which must have been a mindboggling experience!

Philip Stevens has been in the village for 24 years and moved here with Denise having spent a year in the Transkei working in a Mission Hospital with her.

He spends most of his time running a GP practice in Brackley which has doubled in size over that time. However for two weeks every year he takes his holiday back in the Transkei working in the Hospital. He stands in for some of the doctors so that they can have a holiday and goes out into the countryside two days a week giving GP and Nurse training in village clinics within a 60 mile radius. He also takes a 3 month sabbatical every five years and spends the time in South Africa at the Hospital.